# Pressing On in The Spirit

Maria Vadia

## Queenship

**PUBLISHING COMPANY**
P.O. Box 220 • Goleta, CA 93116

Scripture Passages:

The Holy Bible, Ignatius Press, revised standard version, Catholic Edition. Thomas Helson and Son, 1966.

Other Bibles used:

New American Bible, Saint Joseph Edition Catholic Book Publishing Co. New York, 1970.

New King James Version, Spirit Filled Life Bible, 1991 Thomas Nelson. Inc.

New Testament, The Word of God, Alive and Active Today's English Version. American Bible Society, New York, 1992.

The Message, The Bible in Contemporary Language, Peterson, Eugene H. Navpress 2002.

Library of Congress Number #2004093840

Published by:
    Queenship Publishing
    P.O. Box 220
    Goleta, CA 93116
    (800) 647-9882 • (805) 692-0043 • Fax: (805) 967-5133
    www.queenship.org

Printed in the United States of America

ISBN: 1-57918-264-X

# Contents

# Dedication and Thanksgiving

I dedicate this book to our precious Holy Spirit,
our wonderful helper.

I want to thank all those that have prayed
and encouraged me along the way, especially:

My Miami Family:
Fifi, Ina, Cristina, Rene, Valli, Mary, Chris and all the members
of the "King Jesus" prayer group.

My Magnificat sisters around the world.

My African family.

Sister Bernadette Beamsley D.L.J.C. and Fr. Dan Doyle S.M.

# Foreword

Maria Vadia is a true daughter of Abraham, our father in the faith. As a result, she has claimed, is claiming and will claim even more the amazing "promise of inheriting the world".

She, like many renewed Christians, received great promises from God upon her conversion. However, unlike many of us, she was willing to pay the price to come into the inheritance: that is, to sell everything, to pay the price to follow the Holy Spirit's every inspiration, to go through years of testing without looking back, to become a woman of prayer. As a result she has joined the school of brides of the Lamb, following Him with Mother Mary from Galilee to Calvary, and right through. It is as though she no longer belongs to this world, but has "passed over" to resurrection land where her bridegroom lives, and she with Him. She walks among daily miracles, on the wavelength of the Holy Spirit. She lives a continual Pentecost.

You cannot read this book without catching some of that fire, and wanting to have it yourself. It is full of practical wisdom on "how to do it", how to cash in on your personal promises from a loving Father.

The word of God, in which Maria is totally immersed, just comes alive in her life. And it works! Her incredible witness to that is irrefutable, enticing, heart-warming.

In the pages of this book you will find all the keys you need to a more fruitful life in Christ. You will discover that you can live by the promise of Ro. 8, 28, that "for those who love God and are called in His plan, everything works together for good". Everything! You won't have to live by "Murphy's Law" anymore.

Read this book, live it, join this fiery Bride of Christ as we enter a new era of world-changing Christianity.

> Fr. John Randall
> Spirit and the Word Ministry,
> Rhode Island.

# KEEP PRESSING ON!

"Thus says the Lord God. None of my words will be delayed any longer, but the word which I will speak will be performed, says the Lord God." (Ezequiel 12:28).

I have written this book to encourage you to not give up as you wait on God. If the Lord has given you His Word, if He has placed a dream or vision in your heart, it will surely come to pass. You know you're alive for that purpose! Stand on the solid rock of His Word as He uses you to bring forth His purposes. Your muscle of faith will be strengthened and stretched as you wait on Him. There are battles to be fought, fears to be dealt with, cleansings, healings, heartaches and headaches to go through. Count it all as joy! (James 1:2-4)

There is a general plan for humanity: salvation in Jesus! There's a specific plan for your life now that you are in Christ. God has created you, called you and gifted you specifically for this plan. The vision is burning in your heart and you're waiting!

God's delays are part of the program, and He delays for several reasons: to purify and expose our hearts so that we can repent and be conformed to His image; to develop patience and perseverance, to bring glory to the name of Jesus, to get us ready for His blessing and His coming, to sharpen our focus. Our trust must be in Him. "Waiting" is not a waste of time, but a necessary time of preparation for our destiny in Christ. The Lord cares about this journey into our destiny, this time of pressing in, waiting and expecting. He will train "your hands for war, and your fingers for battle" (Ps. 144:1) and will transform you into a true worshipper that worships Him "in spirit and truth." (John 4:23) Joseph and David, among others, had to wait to see God's promises fulfilled in their lives; meditating on their lives has brought much comfort to me when facing delays. David had to wait at least 14 years from the time he was anointed to be king of Israel before he became king of Judah. During that time he had to constantly run for his life because King Saul wanted to kill him. God gave Joseph dreams of greatness; he

*1*

had to endure tremendous sufferings and a long wait before he saw those dreams fulfilled.   It seems that both men had to go through the opposite of what God had promised them before they entered into their destiny.   It's often at this time that many Christians give up.   If you're going through the opposite of what the Lord promised you, this book is for you.   The Scriptures exhort us not to be "sluggish, but imitators of those who through faith and patience inherit the promises" (Hebrews 6:12).   The challenge for us is to keep the fire and passion for Jesus burning in our hearts as we go through the wilderness of waiting.

> "Even youths shall faint and be weary; and young men shall fall exhausted; but they who wait for the Lord shall renew their strength, they shall mount up with wings like eagles, they shall run and not be weary, they shall walk  and not be faint." (Isaiah 40:30-31)

# I. GOD'S DELAYS

"For still the vision awaits its time; it hastens to the end—it will not lie. If it seems slow, wait for it; it will surely come, it will not delay." (Habakkuk 2:3)

## Idolatry exposed

"You shall not have other gods besides me." (Deut. 5:7)

It only took 40 days for the Israelites in the desert to turn to idolatry because "Moses delayed to come down from the mountain..." (Exodus 32:1). Acts 7:39 quotes Stephen as saying that "... in their hearts they turned back to Egypt" (NKJV). Even though they had seen with their eyes God's awesome deliverance from the yoke of Pharaoh, they chose to worship a golden calf instead of the God who had delivered them out of Egypt, the place of bondage. They "exchanged the glory of the immortal God for images resembling mortal man or birds or animals..." (Romans 1:23). Today we don't bow before a golden cow, but idolatry is still rampant. Anything that we put our trust in apart from God can become an idol. The Scriptures reveal that we are cursed if that happens.

Jeremiah 17:5-6 "Thus says the Lord: Cursed is the man who trusts in man and makes flesh his arm, whose heart turns away from the Lord. He is like a shrub in the desert, and shall not see any good come. He will dwell in the parched places of the wilderness, in an uninhabited salt land."

Many people feel empty and fruitless, like "a shrub in the desert," with no meaning and purpose in life. According to the prophet Jeremiah, their trust is in the wrong place. The world teaches us to trust in self, others or the system. The reality is that until we find Jesus and trust in Him, we will not be complete nor satisfied, for it's only in Him that we have "fullness of life" (Colossians 2:10). It is "through Him and for Him" that we were created (Colossians 1:16). Jesus says "I came that they may have life, and have it abundantly" (John 10:10). His will for us is that we bear fruit (John 15:16). The result of idolatry is just disastrous; the Apostle Paul says in Romans 1:24-25:

> "Therefore God gave them up in the lusts of their hearts to impurity, to the dishonoring of their bodies among themselves, because they exchanged the truth about God for a lie and worshipped and served the creature rather than the Creator, who is blessed for ever! Amen."

The truth is that when we are in idolatry God will not only give us up to the "lusts of our hearts to impurity," but also to "dishonorable passions" v.26 and "a base mind and to improper conduct" v.28. Idolatry leads us into a downward spiral of sin: wickedness, evil, covetousness, malice, envy, murder, strife, deceit, malignity, gossip, slander, hatred of God, insolence, haughtiness, boasting; more invention of evil, disobedience to parents, foolishness, faithlessness, heartlessness, ruthlessness (v. 29-31). According to Romans 1:18-32, the root of much of the sin, problems and difficulties that we face today in our families and nation is idolatry! It's interesting to note that after the Israelites created the golden calf, they "rose up early on the morrow, and offered burnt offerings and brought peace offerings (to the calf); and the people sat down to eat and drink, and rose up to play" (Exodus 32:6). The idea here is that they turned away from God and started to indulge in an ungodly way. Verses 7-8 continue "And the Lord said to Moses, go down; for your people, whom you brought up out of the land of Egypt, have corrupted themselves; they have turned aside quickly out of the way which I commanded them...."

We have gone to the wisdom of the world for answers instead of turning to Jesus, Who is the "wisdom of God" (1 Corinthians 1:24). He has stored up "sound wisdom for the upright..." (Proverbs 2:7). The Lord says through the prophet Jeremiah:

"for my people have committed two evils: they have forsaken me, the fountain of living waters, and hewed out cisterns for themselves, broken cisterns, that can hold no water" (Jeremiah 2:13).

How does this apply to ourselves today? It's simple: God in His mercy sent His Son, the Lord Jesus Christ, to redeem a lost humanity out of the hand of the enemy and deliver us from the dominion of darkness into the kingdom of God. It's to Jesus that we owe our lives, our worship, our everything; in spite of this, most of us still live for ourselves and look for answers in the wrong places. There is the worship of self, money, prestige, status; the worship of others; the worship of your job, your reputation or your pension plan; the worship of comfort, alcohol, sex, drugs and of your t.v. set. Some worship psychology. We could even worship our "ministry!" Selfish ambition dominates many peoples' lives. Psychic hot lines are big business! On Sundays many lives revolve around the football games. In my area there is a Sunday Mass many people call the "micro-wave" Mass because it will not interfere with their schedule! It's in and out! Some are so in love with self, that, like King Saul in 1 Samuel 15:12, they erect a monument in their own honor. Whose image are you reflecting, your own or Christ's? Whose kingdom are you building? It's time to smash those idols because our God is a jealous God who will not give His glory to another! (Deut. 4:24)

Jesus says in Matthew 6:24:

"No one can serve two masters; for either he will hate the one and love the other, or he will be devoted to the one and despise the other. You cannot serve God and mammon."

The love of money, rampant in our society, is something the Apostle Paul warns as being "the root of all evils...;" not money itself, but the love of it, and it opens the door to all other evils! (1 Timothy 6:10) Tithing, offerings and gifts to the Lord have the power to prevent money from becoming an idol; they help us to trust God with our finances. Dear reader, if you are not tithing, you will not enter into your "destiny" in this planet. Jesus says in Luke 16:11:

"If then you have not been faithful in the unrighteous mammon, who will entrust to you the true riches?

The Lord is saying that if we can't handle money the right way (His way), He cannot trust us with more important things. For example, if we are not tithing, how can He really trust us with a ministry, with His people, with the anointing, with a "vision," with " the true riches?" If we have not been faithful with the least of the blessings, which is money, how can He trust us with anything else? We must understand that the first ten percent of our income belongs to the Lord. The blessings that come from tithing are many (read Malachi 3:8-12). Special offerings and almsgiving are also dear to the heart of God!

I remember during a time of great financial difficulty in my life when all I had was $40 in my wallet, and I felt rich. I was on my way to see my spiritual director, who was the pastor of a very poor parish. I heard the Lord say "Give him the $40." Immediately I said, "okay"; I had the sense that this money would be for someone who was hungry, not money for transportation or medicine. However, it was a long ride, and my mind started to interfere with what the Lord had asked me to do. It went something like this: "Be smart, give him $20 and keep $20 for yourself; who knows, you might need it for an emergency; after all, you have four kids." By the grace of God, as I parked my car, I said to the Lord "Lord I'm going to give Father Bagan the $40 because I believe that $40 is what I heard; but please let me know if I heard correctly." I went in to the rectory and talked to Father. After hearing my confession I gave him the $40. He looked at the $40 and said to me "Maria, you won't believe this; this morning a poor parishioner of mine called me up saying she was out of a job and that she had no food at the house. She said that if only I could give her $40 to buy food she would be okay for the rest of the week." Needless to say, I left penniless but abounding in the joy of the Lord! I rejoiced in His love and faithfulness. I was so thankful to the Lord that I was able not only to hear His voice and obey it, but that I had been an instrument of blessing for His body. The Lord showed me something that day: if the Church, us, would only listen to His voice, there would be no lack in His body. The same spirit of generosity that permeated the early Church would permeate the church today. It's interesting to note that after the Holy Spirit was poured out on Pentecost, "There was not a needy person among them..." (Acts 4:34).

Our human nature has a tendency to turn to idols even after we have experienced His love, forgiveness and power in our lives. We are prone to placing even a child or spouse in God's place! The Lord warned His people before entering the Promised Land not to forget Him:

> "lest, when you have eaten and are full, had have built goodly houses and live in them, and when your herds and flocks multiply and your silver and gold is multiplied, and all that you have is multiplied, then your heart be lifted up, and you forget the Lord your God, who brought you out of the land of Egypt, out of the house of bondage..." (Deut. 8:12-14). Verses 17-18 continue with the admonition:

> "Beware lest you say in your heart, My power and the might of my hand have gotten me this wealth. You shall remember the Lord your God, for it is he who gives you power to get wealth...."

The Lord makes it clear in His Word that we must continue in a state of dependence and reliance on Him regardless of how success-ful we become, or our "hearts will be lifted up." King Amaziah (2 Chronicles 25:19) had to be rebuked by King Joash after a victory: "...your heart has lifted you up in boastfulness." King Saul had to be rebuked by the prophet Samuel because of his disobedience and prideful spirit: "When you were little in your own eyes, were you not head of the tribes of Israel? And did not the Lord anoint you king over Israel?" (1Samuel 15:17 NKJ). We are to remain "little" in our eyes, knowing that "Every good endowment and every perfect gift is from above..." (James 1:17). Pride leads

7

to our downfall. "Pride goes before destruction, and a haughty
spirit before a fall (Proverbs 16:18). King Uzziah (2 Chronicles
26:15-16) "was marvelously helped, till he was strong. But when
he was strong he grew proud, to his destruction. For he was false
to the Lord his God...." Even a "good" king like Hezekiah became
proud and had to "humble himself for the pride of his heart." (2
Chronicles 32:26) James 4:6 says "God opposes the proud, but
gives grace to the humble." It's your choice to remain proud and
have God oppose you, or to humble yourself before Him and receive
grace. *humble yourself*
    Idolatry must be dealt with; we will not love God wholeheart-
edly if we are gripped by it! It clouds our vision and prevents us
from having a "sound" eye (Matthew 6:22), so necessary in order
to follow Him wholeheartedly through the difficulties and trials
that we must go through in order to make it into our destiny (Acts
14:22). During the time of delay the Lord wants to adjust our
spiritual eyes so that we have 20/20 vision in the Spirit!
    This is how God wants us to deal with our idols:

"But thus shall you deal with them: you shall destroy their
altars, and break down their sacred pillars, and cut down
their wooden images, and burn their carved images with
fire" (Deut. 7:5). (NKJ)

It's in the "delay" that we must break down, destroy, smash,
chop down and burn some things in our lives. These idols in our
lives work somewhat like the "thorns" Jesus talked about in the
parable of the seed. These "thorns" in our hearts are the cares of
the world, the delight in riches, and the desire for other things; they
"choke the Word" and we remain unfruitful (Mark 4:18-19). It's
in that dream, that vision or promise that He has deposited inside
of you, that you will bear much fruit, for the glory of God! Now is
the time to pluck out those thorns! The prophet Jeremiah says:

"Break up your fallow ground, and sow not among thorns.
Circumcise yourselves to the Lord, remove the foreskin of
your hearts...." (4:3)

8

The Apostle Paul commends the Thessalonians because they:

"turned to God from idols, to serve a living and true God,
and to wait for his Son from heaven, whom He raised from
the dead, Jesus who delivers us from the wrath to come."
(1 Thessalonians 1:9-10)

As God's people, we must be lovers of the truth. We must search the Scriptures in the same spirit as the Bereans (Acts 17:11-12), or else we will create our own God according to our ideas and desires, and we will end up worshipping an idol. There won't be any transformation in Christ because we are not "beholding the glory of the Lord" (2 Corinthians 3:18) but a lie and a deception. The Holy Spirit, the spirit of truth (John 14:17), will "guide us into all the truth" (John 16:13). Jesus said: "He will glorify Me..." (John 16:14).

After Saul of Tarsus had an encounter with the risen Lord, he was able to say that he counted everything as "refuse" compared to the "surpassing worth of knowing Christ Jesus my Lord." (Phillipians 3:8) We need a personal encounter with the risen Lord, so that we too can count all as "refuse" when compared to Christ. We must at least get a glimpse of the "treasure" (Matthew 13:44) so that we can leave everything behind in order to follow Him! We, the Bride of Christ, must quit playing "the harlot with many lovers." (Jeremiah 3:1) The spiritual adultery must be broken! Fall in love with Him! *When you fall in love with Jesus you want to spend more time with Him*

Let's pray: "Father, I desire to turn away from my idols and turn to Jesus. I repent from my idolatry and I ask the Holy Spirit, the Spirit of revelation, to reveal to me now those areas in my life where Jesus is not Lord, where I have been trusting in the wrong things. Teach me how to handle money in a way that pleases You. I abandon myself to You. Adjust my vision and give me a love for the truth. Lord Jesus, I want to live for You; take my life and use it for Your glory. Sit on the throne and rule my life. I receive the grace now to make the adjustments I need to make. Come, Holy Spirit, and have Your way in me. Amen!"

A NOTE ON THE OCCULT: It doesn't matter how long it has been since you haven't done it; you must repent and renounce it, with your mouth, out loud. If you have been involved in the occult, you have sought other Gods. Go back to that moment when you opened a door to the enemy, whether through horoscopes, ouija boards, tarot cards, Santeria, New Age, palm reading, etc., and shut that door! A young mother that was coming to Bible class, after realizing how offensive anything occult is to the Lord, confided in me that as a teenager she went together with her friends to visit a Santeria witch. These teenagers wanted boyfriends and decided to try the occult in order to get them. They did as this woman told them to do and visited her a few times. That was the end of that. Now many years later my friend realized that she had never openly renounced it. I led her in a prayer of repentance and renunciation, shutting that door that she haeàopened years ago. She told me later that by the time she got to the parking lot of the Church, she was burping the longest burps, coming from deep within her. This burping continued for a while and afterwards she started to experience such a joy that she went to Mass to celebrate. Whatever had come in years ago came out now in the name of Jesus! Evil spirits often leave us by expelling our breath; burping, coughing, yawning, vomiting, are some of the ways.

My friend Mary had been very involved in yoga and New Age for many years. She followed a guru. After coming to the Lord she started to experience pains in her chest but did not tell anybody. Being a nurse, she thought that it was part of the aging process (a lie from the pit of hell!) and accepted it. One day as she was worshipping the Lord she started to experience excruciating pains in her heart; she asked the Lord about it and He answered "This is satan; he comes to steal, kill, and destroy and he wants you dead." Mary proceeded to take authority over the enemy and spoke the Word of God over her situation. The anointing of the Holy Spirit was on her and she started to burp until she experienced a joy rising up in

her. Since that day she has not experienced any chest pains! Glory
to God! What had come in years earlier through involvement in
the occult now came out through the anointing of the Holy Spirit!
Thank you, Jesus!

## Fears, flesh and more exposed

"Though an army encamp against me, my heart will not
fear; though war be waged upon me, even then will I trust."
(Ps. 27: 3) (NAB)

Before Moses came down from the mountain, Aaron had already buckled to the people's demands. He was a people-pleaser.
He had more fear of man than fear of God. He then lied to Moses
when Moses confronted him with the truth (Exodus 32:21-24).
Aaron was bound by self-protection, fear of man and fear of being
exposed by the truth, not good qualities for leadership!

In Samuel 13, we see King Saul disobeying God, taking matters
into his own hands when Samuel doesn't arrive at just the right time.
Saul waited for Samuel 7 days, the specified time, and when Samuel
didn't arrive just in time, he proceeded to offer up the holocaust
and peace offerings, something that only priests were supposed to
do. Because of his "anxiety" he broke the Lord's command. In
verse 11 we see that Saul was afraid because "the people were
scattering from me...." Instead of turning to the Lord for help
and guidance he let fear and impatience rule his life. Fear is a big
enemy, but the Spirit we have received is not fear but one of power!
(2 Tim. 1:7) Fear entered the world through the disobedience of
our first parents. After they disobeyed God and ate from the Tree
of the Knowledge of Good and Evil, they hid from the presence
of the Lord when they heard the sound of the Lord walking in the
garden.

"But the Lord God called to the man, and said to him,
'Where are you?' And he said, 'I heard the sound of thee
in the garden, and I was afraid, because I was naked; and

*11*

I hid myself'" (Genesis 3:9-10).

Fear caused Adam and Eve to hide from God. As long as we keep eating from the wrong tree we will experience fear and spiritual defeat. Fear is an enemy that can prevent us from entering into our "destiny." Faith, the opposite of fear, causes us to turn to the Lord. When we are afraid, we must learn to face those fears and not give in to them, but rather turn to God. The Lord has a plan! Ps. 56:3-4 says:

"When I am afraid I put my trust in thee,
In God, whose word I praise, In God I trust without a fear.
What can flesh do to me?"

King Jehoshaphat experienced fear when three enemy armies more powerful than his came against Judah, but he "set himself to seek the Lord..." (2 Chronicles 20:3). He turned to the Lord. The outcome was a tremendous victory in an "impossible" situation! Faith won over fear! The Lord gave him the strategy for victory. The enemy loves to release fear against us. He knows that when we are afraid we may easily fall into the trap of self-protection and impatience, causing us to take matters into our own hands and make the wrong moves. We move out of God's protection when we "decide" to take action motivated by our fears (like King Saul). This happened to our patriarchs Abraham, Isaac and Jacob when faced by fears. They had a problem with lying because of fear (Genesis 12:11-20; Genesis 20:2-18; Genesis 26:7; Genesis 27). They used lying and deception when afraid instead of waiting and trusting God. This is why the Apostle Paul tells us to "...walk by the Spirit, and do not gratify the desires of the flesh." (Galatians 5:16) Flesh-based decisions will always get us in trouble and will not produce good fruit. Look at what happened to Sarai and Abram when she became impatient waiting for the promised son; the fruit of Sarai's "plan" was Ishmael, while the fruit of the promise was Isaac. These two cannot co-exist; for the son born "according to the flesh persecuted him who was born according to the Spirit..."

(Galatians 4:29). When we think of the strife and the many divisions in the Church, could it be because of so many Ishmaels being conceived in the flesh rather than Isaacs in the Spirit?

Is your life marked with little Ishmaels or Isaacs?

I remember when the Lord called me to the prison ministry. I became impatient and made my own plans as to how I would go to the prison, rather than ask the Lord how this would be accomplished. I called a priest I knew that went to the prison and asked him to take me with him. But this was not God's plan. It never worked out because of conflicts in our schedules. Frustration set in. However, at just the right time, when I gave up my own plans, the Lord intervened. Just around that time my sister invited to our prayer group a lady she met at the Blessed Sacrament chapel. It was a divine appointment. Unknown to us, this lady was the person in charge of Catholic prison ministry for the Women's Detention Center. After a few visits to our prayer group, she walked up to me and invited me to preach on Saturdays at the women's jail. I knew immediately that the Lord who had called me to prison ministry was providing the way. When He calls, He provides! I've been preaching at the women's jail for the last ten years! The lesson to be learned is to quit taking action and making decisions motivated by our flesh. We must allow the Holy Spirit to guide us and reveal to us God's plan. The Lord has the perfect timing.

"And your ears shall hear a word behind you, saying, This is the way, walk in it, when you turn to the right or when your turn to the left." (Isaiah 30:21)

God, who is in control of our lives, wants to have His purpose and plan fulfilled in our lives. He wants to take us into our "destiny." We are our biggest problems! Self-centeredness, self-will, selfishness, self-reliance, self-sufficiency, self-promotion are things that need to be broken so that we can become Christ-centered, as God had originally intended. This transformation takes place by the power of the Holy Spirit as we repent of our sins and Jesus

*13*

becomes the Lord of our lives. Allow the Lord to deal with your secret sins; allow Him to expose wrong motives in your life! It is the goal of the Holy Spirit to create Christ in us. The Apostle Paul tells the church in Galatia:

"My little children, with whom I am again in travail until Christ be formed in you!" (Galatians 4:19).

Could it be that during this time of "delay" the Lord wants to see Christ formed in you? "Is the fruit of the Holy Spirit manifested in your life?" (Galatians 5:22-23) Whatever does not line up with the fruit of the Holy Spirit must die!

I John 2:6 says that:

"he who says he abides in Him ought to walk in the same way in which He walked."

Can we walk like He walked? By the power of the Holy Spirit we can! The Word of God says to! We must consider ourselves "dead to sin and alive to God in Christ Jesus." (Romans 6:11) His grace is sufficient for us; He says:

"My power is made perfect in weakness" (2 Corinthians 12:9).

Take a look at those "weak areas" and believe that His grace is available for you to overcome sin and to walk like "He walked." 1 Corinthians 6:19-20 says:

"Do you not know that your body is a temple of the Holy Spirit within you, which you have from God? You are not your own; you were bought with a price. So glorify God in your body."

Since we don't belong to ourselves any longer, we live for Him and in a way that glorifies Him. Even our bodies belong to Him now! Jesus will not come back for a filthy bride. He will come back for one "without spot or wrinkle or any such thing, that she might be holy and without blemish." (Ephesians 5:27) We want His will in every situation. Jesus said in John 4:34:

"My food is to do the will of him who sent me, and to finish his work." (NKJ)
Is that your food?

Let's pray: "Father, I want Christ to be formed in me. Holy Spirit, I give you permission to change me and transform me into the image of Jesus. I want the fruit of Your Spirit to be manifested in my life. Give me the grace to seek His kingdom first in every situation. Lord, I trust You with my life. I want to live controlled by your Spirit and not by my flesh. I receive now the grace I need to get rid of sin and not to compromise with it. In Jesus' name, I pray. Amen."

## Our state of readiness exposed

"Be on guard, therefore. The Son of Man will come when you least expect him." (Luke 12:40) (NAB)

As you know, Jesus has promised to return, and He will return unexpectedly, like a thief in the night. When He comes back He wants to find "faithful and wise" servants in His household. (Matthew 24:45). He has commanded His people to "Go therefore and make disciples of all nations..." (Matthew 28:19-20). The Great Commission is not the great omission! All of God's people are supposed to GO with the "good news" of the gospel wherever He tells us. This command is for all believers, not just for a "select" few. No matter what specific plan or "destiny" the Lord has for each one of us, we're also supposed to proclaim the Gospel wherever we go. So we do both; we participate in the proclamation of the Gospel and in His specific plan that He has for each one of us. Maybe the Lord has called you to feed the hungry under the bridge, visit the sick, teach the learning disabled or help orphans; you're also supposed to share the good news as well. If not, it's social work! My friend Cristina is married to a doctor. She works part time in his office; as she does, she prays with his patients for healing and leads them to Jesus. She gives them Bibles and salvation tracts. My friend Gilda, a social worker, has pointed many of her clients to Jesus and sends them to retreats and prayer groups. Suzy, a schoolteacher, has led many of her students to Jesus. I hear many Catholics say that "evangelization" is not for them. Wrong! It's at the heart of the Church. It's Jesus' idea! Pope Paul VI said that the Church "exists to evangelize". Who is the Church? US! Get rid of the "I'm not called" mentality and get on with God's plan of salvation, "For the harvest is plentiful, but the laborers are few! (Matthew 9:37) When was the last time that you shared with somebody the good news of salvation in Christ Jesus? When was the last time you led someone to Jesus? Do you know how many people don't have a clue that salvation is a gift from God? Or worse, they think everyone is saved! Remember, God:

"desires all men to be saved and to come to the knowledge of the truth. For there is one God, and there is one mediator between God and men, the man Christ Jesus, who gave himself as a ransom for all..." (1 Timothy 2:4-6).

We're not saved by osmosis. Someone needs to proclaim the truth of the gospel to people so they can repent and turn to Jesus. (This means you have to open your mouth and speak!) Someone has to do it! It's you! "...it pleased God through the folly of what we preach to save those who believe." (1 Cor. 1:21b) Look at what the Apostle Paul says in Romans 10:13-15:

"For every one who calls upon the name of the Lord will be saved. But how are men to call upon Him in whom they have not believed? And how are they to believe in Him of whom they have never heard? And how are they to hear without a preacher? And how can men Preach unless they are sent?"

But we have been sent! Jesus said in Matthew 28:19 "GO..."! Aren't you glad that Jesus told the Father "I'll GO!"

Writing about the Lord's second coming, Peter says in 2 Peter 3:9:

"The Lord does not delay in keeping his promise—though some consider it delay. Rather, He shows you generous patience, since He wants none to perish but all to come to repentance." (NAB)

We must understand the "heart" of God: He wants "none to perish!" The eternal perspective must become real to us; our hearts need to break with compassion for the lost knowing that if they don't repent of their sins and turn to Jesus they cannot receive forgiveness and salvation. Once I understood this, my shyness left! Looking like a "fool" in front of others (1 Corinthians 4:10) is worth it if just one person repents and turns to the Lord!

Many of His parables in the gospels exhort us to get ready to meet Him. We usually don't pay much attention to being ready, but the fact is that Jesus tells us to watch and to be alert more often than we would like to hear. In the parable of the ten virgins in Matthew 25, the groom (Jesus) delayed and the state of unreadiness of the five foolish virgins cost them their entrance into the wedding feast. The foolish virgins, even though they smelled good and looked good, had not developed a personal relationship with Jesus. He told them in v. 12 "...I do not know you." They didn't have eternal life even though they attended church! Jesus Himself gives the definition of eternal life in John 17:3:

"And this is eternal life, that they know thee the only true God, and Jesus Christ whom thou has sent."

Do you know Him?

These foolish virgins had no intimacy with the Lord; they had not been in fellowship with Him, breaking and partaking of

17

the bread of His Word. They had not gone into His presence to be "anointed with fresh oil." (Ps. 92:10) (NKJ) It's daily that we need to go into the Lord's presence, and be anointed with "fresh oil," for we cannot live today with yesterday's grace. We need to hear His voice daily to stay on track. Please don't tell me that on Sunday Mass you "listen" to the Scripture readings. That's like being spoonfed once a week! How can we possibly live with one meal per week? How can we move in power and boldness to proclaim the Gospel if we don't spend time with the Lord? When the religious authorities saw the boldness of Peter and John,

"they recognized that they had been with Jesus."
(Acts 4:13)

As Catholics, we have the great blessing of Blessed Sacrament chapels, where we can virtually be set apart with God to commune with Him. Make use of them!

"The groom delayed his coming, so they all began to nod,
then to fall asleep." (Matthew 25:5) (NAB)

I believe that's the state of the church: ASLEEP! It's our responsibility to stay awake! It's hard to stay awake when we're just sitting on the pew of the Church! We're supposed to "GO"! We're not spectators! We are the army of the Lord! The Church is packed with "foolish virgins" who still need to repent! The Church is God's representative on planet earth; He has empowered us and given us His authority to extend His kingdom, to open the eyes of the blind, to set the captives free, to destroy the works of the devil. The gospel "is the power of God for salvation to every one who has faith..." (Romans 1:16). Jesus said in John 14:12:

"Truly, truly, I say to you, he who believes in me
will also do the works that I do; and greater works
than these will he do, because I go to the Father."

Healings, miracles, signs and wonders followed the ministry of

Jesus, and these follow us as we rise up and "GO." He said "greater works" we would do! As a matter of fact, the early church prayed for the power of the Holy Spirit to be released powerfully:

> "...grant to thy servants to speak thy word with all bold-ness, while thou stretchest out thy hand to heal, and signs and wonders are performed through the name of thy holy servant Jesus"(Acts 4:29-30).

Jesus said in Mark (16:15-18) when He commanded us to preach the Gospel to every creature, that there would be signs that would follow us as we proclaim the Gospel:

> "In "In my Name th
> cast out demons; they will speak
> in new tongues; they will pick up serpents, and if they
> drink any deadly thing it will not hurt them; they will lay
> their hands on the sick and they will recover."

These signs followed the disciples as they obeyed the Lord Jesus. "And they went forth and preached everywhere, while the Lord worked with them and confirmed the message by the signs that attended it." (v.20). THEY WENT FORTH! We must go forth too! And as we do, these signs will follow us too! For example, when the Lord used Peter and John to heal the crippled beggar (Acts 3), this one miracle of healing brought in 5,000 converts! Signs and wonders are important: they point to "King Jesus" and help to bring people to repentance. The Pharisees and chief priests got worried when they heard Jesus had raised Lazarus from the dead.

> "What are we to do? For this man performs many signs. If we let Him go on thus, every one will believe in Him...." (John 11:48)

We are supposed "to walk in the same way in which He walked"

(1John 2:6); in the power of the Holy Spirit! Acts 10:38 says:

"how God anointed Jesus of Nazareth with the
Holy Spirit and with power; how he went about
doing good and healing all that were oppressed
by the devil, for God was with Him."

We too have been anointed with the Holy Spirit and with power!
We too are to do good and bring healing to the oppressed; God is
with us! We are to remain abiding in Him, for apart from Him
we "can do nothing" (John 15:5). I want to show you how easy
it is to bring healing to others. In one Bible class a young mother
had a toothache and needed a root canal. I asked her if I could
pray for her and laid my hand on her. I must admit she was a little
"surprised" as I ministered to her. Two weeks later her tooth was
completely healed and did not need a root canal. The dentist said
"It's a miracle!" Now she is also laying hands on others for healing! My brother Rene, a doctor, has just experienced a conversion
to Jesus Christ. He's not wasting any time. He's already laying
hands on his patients for Jesus to heal them. Daily he has praise
reports of God's healing power. Recently he laid hands on someone who had a huge tumor on her pancreas. My brother asked her
"Do you believe in Jesus Christ?" The lady said she did. They
prayed. When she went to have a biopsy done that same day, there
was nothing on her pancreas! Bringing healing to others is normal
Christianity! It's the power of the Gospel being demonstrated. It
doesn't matter where you are; you take the Holy Spirit with you
wherever you go! Jesus is the healer and we are His instruments.
The Apostle Paul says that "we are His workmanship, created in
Christ Jesus for good works, which God prepared beforehand, that
we should walk in them." (Ephesians 2:10) Good works cannot
save us, but our good works have already been chosen and prepared by God for us. These are the "good works" connected to our
destiny, to the vision He has placed in our hearts. It's time to rise
up and start walking in them! The Apostle John says in Revelation
19:7-8:

"Let us rejoice and exult and give Him the glory, for the marriage of the Lamb has come, and His Bride has made herself ready; it was granted her to be clothed with fine linen, bright and pure, for the fine linen is the righteous deeds of the saints."

Are you getting dressed with "fine linen?"
Some people allow their troubles and difficulties to rule their lives. Instead of "walking by faith" (2 Corinthians 5:7) they allow their circumstances to control them. They wait for that "difficulty-free" and "problem-free" time in order to serve the Lord. Needless to say, they will never serve God because there will always be hassles, difficulties and troubles; the Lord has allowed these troubles so that we learn to persevere and breakthrough to victory! We must learn to overcome the strategies of the enemy. Having a clear vision of our mission and destiny will help us stay on track no matter what comes against us. We need vision for the mission because there is a desert to go through before entering our destiny. Jesus said in John 16:33:

"In the world you have tribulation; but be of good cheer, I have overcome the world."

Jesus also said in Matthew 10:8(b) "You received without pay, give without pay." He didn't say to freely give IF your life was in perfect order. What needs to be in order is your heart! Get your heart right with God! It has been my own personal experience that as I persevered during trials and difficulties to serve God no matter what, I was invariably blessed as I served Him. The Holy Spirit ministered to me as I ministered to others. That's why Jesus said "It is more blessed to give than to receive" (Acts 20:35), because when you give you receive. Proverbs 11:25(b) says:

"and one who waters will himself be watered."

Don't believe the lie of the enemy that you can't serve Him until your life is "perfect." Just get your heart right with Him and move on in the power of the Holy Spirit to be His witness and to do the good works He has chosen for you. When Jesus comes back and He starts to separate the sheep from the goats, on which side will you be? (Matthew 25:31-46)

Let's pray: Father, I thank You that I belong to You and that You have a life of good works already prepared for me. I believe that if You chose me You have given me the anointing I need to fulfill Your purposes. Holy Spirit, open the eyes of my understanding and help me believe that there is a specific plan for my life. Release Your power in my life and show me where I belong in Your body. Use me also to proclaim Your gospel with boldness and that signs and wonders follow me as I do. Lord, I choose Your destiny for my life. I pray in Jesus' name, Amen.

# His glory is revealed

"Did I not tell you that if you would believe you would see the glory of God displayed? (John 11:40)

When Jesus' friend Lazarus was sick, Jesus took His time. (John:11) His sisters even sent word to Him, but Jesus delayed. By the time He got to Bethany, Lazarus was already dead four days. His own disciples didn't quite understand what was going on. But isn't a resurrection more glorious than a healing? Wasn't God's glory manifested big time through Lazarus' resurrection? This delay took place to display the power of God. When everyone thought it was all over, here comes Jesus and resurrects Lazarus.

Remember Jairus, the big shot from the synagogue (Mark 5:22-43)? He asks Jesus to come and heal his daughter, who "is at the point of death." Jesus goes with him. A "delay" takes place, for a woman who had been bleeding for twelve years and who was desperate to get well touches Jesus' garment, in an attempt to get healed. (Mark 5:28) The Bible says that she had "suffered much" with doctors and "was no better but rather grew worse." When she touched Jesus' garment her hemorrhage immediately stopped!

Jesus knew that "power had gone forth from him" and he looked for the person that had touched Him. Finally the woman identified herself and Jesus ministered to her. Jesus took His time. In the meantime, Jairus was still waiting and messengers came with a "negative report". They told him "Your daughter is dead. Why trouble the teacher any further?" (v.35) Isn't it amazing how the devil manages to bring the "negative report" at the worst times? Thank God for Jesus! "But IGNORING WHAT THEY SAID, Jesus said to the ruler of the synagogue

" DO NOT FEAR, ONLY BELIEVE." (Mark 5:36)

When they got to the house there was a big commotion, "people weeping and wailing loudly." I imagine they were having a funeral, but Jesus disrupted it! Jesus took the girl's hand and spoke to her 'Little girl, I say to you, arise.' And immediately the girl got up and walked..." (v.41-42). During this "delay" two miraculous healings took place! The Lord got "double" glory! In both cases the human report was a "negative report"; but both times God's plan prevailed and He was glorified! There's nothing like the power of God to silence the critics!

Sometimes our dreams, visions and projects have to "die" through a delay so that the Lord Himself brings them back to life with great power and glory to His name. It was in 1987 that I was "gloriously" saved and baptized in the Holy Spirit. I knew that the Lord had a plan for my life that was quite different from anything I had imagined. I knew that I couldn't be a "Sunday" Catholic anymore. I had a burning desire to tell others about Jesus and His salvation, and when I did, there was a joy unspeakable! Somehow I knew that I was alive to proclaim the Gospel. "...woe to me if I do not preach the gospel!" (1 Corinthians 9:16) A well-known priest prophesied over me and told me that the Lord was going to use me in ways that I never even imagined. I received that prophetic word with confidence, because I knew in my heart that what he had spoken over my life was true. It agreed with my spirit and I experienced a release of joy when he prophesied. I knew God had spoken through Him. Little did I know then how much I would go through before entering into my "destiny." Little did I know then that it would take over 12 years for me to start entering into the great things that God had planned for my life. (1 Corinthians 2:9) For a while it seemed as if God had forgotten about me! I looked like anything but blessed by God: a broken marriage, abandoned, no money. But the waiting was worth it; He came through! What a joy to see the Lord's word fulfilled! By the grace of God I believed and persevered as I waited. And as I waited many people have turned to Jesus through me. The Lord has now taken me to different continents and nations to proclaim His Word with signs following. (Mark 16:15-18) You see, as we become His witnesses, first in our homes, towns, cities, nations, He will expand His spheres of influence through us "to the end of the earth" just like He told His disciples in Acts 1:8. Little did I know that I would be writing books and speaking in conferences. I look at myself and I am in awe of God, because I was the least likely candidate to be used by Him. As the Apostle Paul says in 1 Cor. 1: 27,

> "God chose those whom the world considers absurd
> to shame the wise; he singled out the weak of this
> world to shame the strong." (NAB)

And in this He is greatly glorified!

Think of Abraham and Sarah waiting for the promise of Isaac. When Abraham was 75 years old God told him that he would make of him a "great nation" (Genesis 12:2) . He waited and waited. Years passed and he continued to be childless (Genesis 15:2). The Lord promised him that his descendants would be as many as the number of the stars (v.5). Finally, when Abraham was 99 years old (Genesis 17) the Lord appeared to him and told him he would be the father of a multitude of nations. The Bible says about Abraham in Romans 4:19-21:

> "He did not weaken in faith when he considered his own
> body, which was as good as dead because he was about a
> hundred years old, or when he considered the barrenness
> of Sarah's womb. No distrust made him waver concerning

the promise of God, but he grew strong in his faith as he gave glory to God, fully convinced that God was able to do what he had promised."

Can you picture Abraham and Sarah, old, wrinkled, no teeth, sitting on their rocking chairs, talking about "the promise" and waiting for him? We must learn that as we "give glory to God" in the waiting we grow strong in faith, just like Father Abraham. Our focus becomes sharpened! The birth of Isaac after such a delay gave great glory to God because it showed that Isaac's birth was the result of God's promise, not the result of man's effort. Abraham's situation was, humanly speaking, hopeless and impossible; in the natural they couldn't have any children. But then came the promise! God is faithful to His Word! Abraham dared to believe God's promise "fully convinced that God was able to do what He had promised," in spite of the fact that their bodies were as "good as dead." This is walking by faith! He focused on what God could do, not on what he couldn't do! It takes believing, especially through a delay, to see the glory of God!

God is greatly glorified through His plan of salvation for humanity. (John 3:16) God's people waited thousands of years for the Redeemer, Jesus Christ.

"But when the time had fully come, God sent forth His Son, born of woman, born under the law, to redeem those who were under the law, so that we might receive adoption as sons." (Galatians 4:4)

All the glory for our salvation goes to Him, precisely because we can't save ourselves. All we can do is humble ourselves before Him and receive what Jesus has already done for us through His death and resurrection. Paul says in Romans 5:6 "While we were yet helpless, at the right time Christ died for the ungodly." God's sense of timing is quite different than ours; what to us is a "delay" for Him is "the right time."

"For everything there is a season, and a time for every

matter under heaven…" (Ecclesiastes 3:1)

Let's pray: "Lord, I believe, help my unbelief! Teach me and help me to walk with You moment by moment, knowing that You are in complete control of every detail in my life. Holy Spirit, create in me the "eyes of an eagle" so that I can see from Your perspective and am able to focus correctly on God's vision and plan for my life. Open my ears, for I desire to hear Your voice and do Your will. Lord, help me to keep pressing on. I want to bring glory to You, Lord Jesus. Amen."

# II. DURING DELAYS

"Therefore do not throw away your confidence, which
has          a great reward.
For you have need of endurance, so that you may do the
    will of God
And receive what is promised.  For yet a little while, and
    the coming one
Shall come and shall not tarry; but my righteous one
shall                 live by faith,
And if he shrinks back, my soul has no pleasure in him."
    (Hebrews 10:35-38).

## GO AND HIDE: ABIDE!

"Be merciful to me, O God, be merciful to me, for in thee
my soul takes refuge; in the shadow of thy wings I will take
refuge, till the storms of destruction pass by." (Ps. 57:1)

In Samuel 19, King Saul is determined to kill David.  Jonathan,
king Saul's son, who loved David "as his own soul" (1 Samuel
18:1), tells David:

"Saul my father seeks to kill you; therefore take heed to
yourself in the morning, stay in a secret place and hide
yourself..."  (1 Samuel 19:2).

It is so important to find "the secret place," where no matter what
is going on around us we have the peace, joy and protection of
the Lord.  "The secret place" is the presence of the Lord, it's that
place of intimacy with Jesus,  it's that place of trust and obedience
where every door and window is shut to the enemy; it's to live and
walk in the Spirit. It's abiding in Him.  Remember, David had been
anointed to be king of Israel and here he was, running for his life!
Proverbs 18:10 says:

"The name of the Lord is a strong tower; the righteous man runs into it and is safe."

We need to reach that point in our lives where Jesus Himself becomes everything to us. He must become our habitation, "for in Him we live and move and have our being..." (Acts 17:28). This is the place where we are "plugged in" to the Holy Spirit. Ps. 91 is full of powerful promises for the believer, but the condition is to "dwell in the shelter of the Most High" and to "abide in the shadow of the Almighty." When we do so, the Lord becomes our refuge and fortress; our deliverer and protector! He says that:

"A thousand may fall at your side, ten thousand at your right hand; but it will not come near you."(Ps. 91:7)

What a promise! In the midst of terrorist attacks we can be confident of His protection! How do you think the Virgin Mary was protected as she "went in haste into the hill country" to visit her cousin Elizabeth (Luke 1:39) considering that it was 90 miles that she had to walk? Mary had made the Lord her habitation and her protection; she trusted in Him completely and went forth without focusing on the danger of the journey. Mary was only a young lady, but she was a doer of the Word! She "abided in the shadow of the Almighty." (Ps. 91:1) I would not allow my daughter to walk day and night 90 miles through Miami even if you paid me, but Mary had heard from God and obeyed, knowing that she was in His perfect will for her life. Ps. 32:7 says:

"Thou art a hiding place for me,
thou preservest me from trouble;
thou dost encompass me with deliverance."

Mary knew this, therefore she was able to "walk by faith" in obedience to the Lord.

It's just amazing when we read about the wreck of Paul's ship off the coast of Malta and how he was able to remain "cool" in the midst of the storm and confusion in the ship (Acts 27). But Paul knew the secret of living in the Spirit! He had made Jesus his habitation! It touches my heart how "he took bread, and giving thanks to God in the presence of all, he broke it and began to eat." (v.35) Paul was able to keep his peace, for he had heard from God, Who had assured him that he would reach Rome safely (Acts 27:24). After the shipwreck they landed in Malta, and Paul ministered healing to all the natives who were sick! (Acts 28:8-9). Nothing could keep Paul down! Signs and wonders followed him!

In the Book of Daniel, chapter 3, there is the amazing story of the three Hebrew young men who would not worship idols or bow down to them. As punishment they ended up in the fiery furnace, which had been heated up seven times hotter than usual. These men praised the Lord in the fiery furnace! They didn't grumble, curse or complain! The Lord Himself came into the furnace with them! In verse 25 the King says "...I see four men loose, walking in the midst of the fire, and they are not hurt; and the appearance of the fourth is like a son of the gods." The King saw with his own eyes that God Himself was with the three men! God Himself met them in the fiery furnace and protected them: "the fire had not had any power over the bodies of those men; the hair of their heads was not singed, their mantles were not harmed and no smell of fire had come upon them." Isn't this powerful? Are you in the fire? Have you made Jesus your habitation, your place of refuge and your strong tower? If you have, He is with you in the midst of the fire; you will come out unharmed and smelling like a rose, just like the three Hebrews. The best part is that after this trial "by fire" they were promoted! It's all about promotion! The Lord wants to place you in a new level of authority!

Recently I had to appear in court for five hours before the judge. I had prayed and fasted, asking the Lord that this legal case would not reach that far. I had prayed for a peaceful settlement that never materialized. I didn't want to go to court. But the Lord, in His mercy, gave me His Word that He was with me:

"But the Lord is with me as a dread warrior; therefore my persecutors will stumble, they will not overcome me. They will be greatly shamed, for they will not succeed."

(Jeremiah 20:11)

I walked into that courtroom "abiding in the shadow of the Almighty" (Ps. 91:1); the Lord kept me in "perfect peace" (Isaiah 26:3) as I answered the questions asked. All I know is that in my weakness, His grace was sufficient. The apostle Paul says in 2 Cor. 12:9,

"...I will all the more gladly boast of my weaknesses, that the power of Christ may rest upon me."

When the judge's ruling came, he ruled in my favor. Thank you, Jesus!

"Therefore the Lord waits to be gracious to you; therefore he exalts himself to show mercy to you. for the Lord is a God of justice; blessed are all Those who wait for Him." (Isaiah 30:18)

# BE TEACHABLE!

"...Come, let us go up to the mountain of the Lord, to the house of the God of Jacob; that he may teach us his ways and that we may walk in his paths." (Isaiah 2:3)

During this time of waiting or "delay" the Lord wants to teach us His ways, because His ways are different from ours (Isaiah 55:8). Let's face it, we need to change and adapt to Him and His ways; it's not the other way around. As God's people we need to be shaped by His Word and not by the world. Moses was right on when he told the Lord:

"Now therefore, I pray thee, if I have found favor in thy sight, Show me now thy ways, that I may know Thee and
find favor in thy sight." (Exodus 33:13)

Moses was not an uneducated person; as a matter of fact, he "was instructed in all the wisdom of the Egyptians, and he was mighty in his words and deeds" (Acts 7:22). However, he had to spend 40 years in the desert getting acquainted with God in order to be used by God in such a mighty way. He couldn't lead God's people with just the "wisdom of the Egyptians!" He had to be taught by God. Moses had a great hunger and desire for God; he desired intimacy with the Lord, unlike the Israelites who didn't want to get too close. "And the people stood afar off, while Moses drew near to the thick darkness where God was." (Exodus 20:21) This is why Ps. 103:7 says:

"He made known his ways to Moses, his acts to the people of Israel."

I remember when I committed my life to the Lord Jesus that I soon realized that I needed (and desired!) to get to know Him and His ways. I knew the ways of the world, even though I was a "Catholic." In my ignorance of God's ways and of the Word of

God, I had believed the lies told by the world. I believed, for example, that abortion was okay if done within the first trimester of the baby's life. I was told that there was no life in the first three months of the baby's life and I believed it. Therefore, when I got pregnant very soon after my second son was born, I proceeded to have an abortion because I just "couldn't deal with another pregnancy!" Imagine my state of shock when after coming to the Lord I realized what I had done: I had killed my own child! However, no matter how great the sin, God's mercy and forgiveness are even greater! There is now " no condemnation" for me because I'm in Christ Jesus (Romans 8:1) and have been cleansed by His precious Blood (Hebrews 9:22). Amen!

God's way is to "live by the Spirit" (Galatians 5:25). "It's not by might nor by power, but by My Spirit says the Lord of hosts"(Zechariah 4:6). It was the Holy Spirit that gave me a hunger for the Word of God and a desire to live in a manner pleasing to Him; this desire did not come from my sinful nature! It was the Holy Spirit that gave me the desire to hear the voice of God, so that I could be a doer of His Word (James 1:22). The Holy Spirit reveals to us the things of God; He is the spirit of wisdom and revelation (Ephesians 1:17). "For the Spirit searches everything, even the depths of God." (1 Cor. 2:10) The Holy Spirit is God's remedy for the Church and the world; however so many of us live as "orphans," as if we didn't have an awesome helper that is just like Jesus! (John 14:16-18) Jesus said "He (the Holy Spirit) will teach you all things... (John 14:26). We have the best teacher to teach us God's ways! God Himself! In Psalm 25:4-5 David says:

"Make me to know thy ways, O Lord;
teach me thy paths. Lead me in thy truth,
and teach me, for thou art the God of my
salvation; for thee I wait all the day long."

Do you know that you can attend Church and not be teachable? Do you know that you can be "religious" and be unteachable? The Pharisees were the most religious of God's people; yet, when Jesus came they killed Him. They had hardened hearts. Look at what Stephen told them in Acts 7:51-52:

"You stiff-necked people, uncircumcised in heart and ears, you always resist the Holy Spirit. As your fathers did, so do you. Which of the prophets did not your fathers persecute? And they killed those who announced beforehand the coming of the Righteous One...."

Jesus told them, "Assuredly, I say to you that tax collectors and harlots enter the kingdom of God before you" (Matthew 21:31).

Are you willing to change, to let go of your agenda, to make adjustments, to give up what is incompatible with the Lord? Have you reached that point in your life that you tell the Lord, "Whatever it takes, Lord!" Then you will hear His voice and He will teach you His ways.

"And your ears shall hear a word behind you, saying,
This is the way, walk in it, when you turn to the right
or when you turn to the left." (Isaiah 30:21)

What made David, the shepherd boy, different from all the men of Israel's army? What did he know, what did he possess, that enabled him to fight Goliath the giant, while "All the men of Israel, when they saw the man, fled from him, and were much afraid?" (1Samuel 17:24) David had not wasted his time as a young shepherd boy; night after night, alone in the backside of the desert, he had developed a relationship with His God and God had taught him His ways. Now he was able to tell the king

"Your servant used to keep sheep for his father; and when there came a lion, or a bear, and took a lamb from the flock, I went after him and smote him and delivered it out of his mouth; and if he arose against me, I caught him by his beard, and smote him and killed him. Your servant has killed both lions and bears; and this uncircumcised Philistine shall be like one of them, seeing he has defied the armies of the living God.... The Lord who delivered me

*33*

from the paw of the lion and from the paw of the bear, will deliver me from the hand of the Philistine." (v.34-37)

David had learned God's ways; he had learned to trust and depend on the Lord as he shepherded his father's flocks, and now he knew that he could count on the Lord to defeat this enemy giant that had come against God's people. David had to learn first how to overcome the lion and the bear in order to fight a Goliath. David told the giant in v.46-47:

"This day the Lord will deliver you into my hand, and I will strike you down and cut off your head...that all the earth may know that there is a God in Israel, and that all this assembly may know that the Lord saves not with sword and spear; for the battle is the Lord's and he will give you into our hand."

David knew that victory came from the Lord, not from "earthly" weapons! David had no fear because the Lord was with him (Ps. 27:1). He was able to face the enemy with great boldness as he trusted in his God. Proverbs 28:1b says "...but the righteous are bold as a lion." No matter what we are going through or how long the delay, the Holy Spirit (our Teacher) is with us and wants to teach and reveal to us the strategy for victory.

"Blessed be the Lord, my rock, who trains my hands for war, and my fingers for battle..." (Ps. 144:1)

In order to move to the next level in God, we must learn what He is trying to teach us now. David could not have faced Goliath if before he had not overcome the lion and the bear. What are the lions and the bears in your life? The Lord says in Ps. 32:8-9:

"I will instruct you and teach you the way you should go;
I will counsel you with my eye upon you. Be not like
a horse or a mule, without understanding, which must

be curbed with bit and bridle, else it will not keep with you."

The Israelites in the desert never entered into their destiny on earth, the Promised Land, even though the Lord had delivered them from bondage in Egypt and it was His desire for them to possess the Land. They refused to trust God and instead grumbled and complained. They refused to learn God's ways and "with most of them God was not pleased...." (1 Cor.10:5)

"For forty years I loathed that generation, and said, they are a people who err in heart, and they do not regard my ways. Therefore I swore in my anger that they should not enter my rest." (Ps. 95:10-11)

The letter to the Hebrews clearly admonishes us to not harden our hearts. Three times in chapters three and four the Holy Spirit says:

"Today, when you hear His voice, do not harden your hearts...." (Hebrews 3:7,15; 4:7)

To have a hardened heart means that you refuse to hear what the Lord wants to tell you; you become stubborn and not docile to the Holy Spirit. You are not willing to let go of your agenda or of your own plans. Many times we are involved in a lot of good works that were not initiated by the Holy Spirit. Many times the good is the enemy of the best! Just because it is a "good" work does not mean that it is a "God" work. The enemy loves to keep God's people busy and entertained with a lot of good stuff without taking time to listen to His voice as to what He really wants; therefore we can miss His purpose and plan for us! To seek His face with a desire to hear His voice, so that we can be a doer of His Word and be in His perfect will for us should be our desire. The Psalmist says in Ps. 130:5-6:

"I wait for the Lord, my soul waits, and in His Word I do

hope my soul waits for the Lord more than watchmen for the morming, more than watchmen for the morning."

Years ago when my sister and I returned from a trip to the Holy Land, our mom told us that our younger brother was hospitalized; he had gone to the hospital to have some tests done. It didn't sound serious. Robert, my brother, didn't know Jesus personally; he needed to be reconciled to God. Several times he had rejected our invitation to get right with God. I had my week planned and organized, all with good stuff. I was planning to visit my brother in the hospital at my convenience. However, during morning Mass, as I listened to the Scriptures, I felt the Lord saying to me to drop my agenda and go straight to the hospital instead. By the grace of God I did just as He told me; I let go of my good plans for God's plans! It was with a lot of caution that I went to see Robert, not even knowing if he would be glad to see me. But it was that morning that Robert repented and gave his life to Jesus! He opened his heart to the Lord and Jesus became his Lord and Savior. It was the perfect timing of the Lord, as my brother passed on to be with the Lord two weeks later. I can look back and know that it was the Holy Spirit who opened my ears, spoke into my heart and guided me out of my "comfort zone" so that God's will could be accomplished in my brother's life. Ps. 40:6 says:

"Sacrifice and offering thou dost not desire; but thou hast given me an open ear."

In Ghana, West Africa, I was preaching one night at a Church and I sensed the Lord telling me to tell the people to start rejoicing and dancing in His presence, and as they did, they would be healed. The people danced and rejoiced and the Lord stretched His arm to heal His people. There were many testimonies of healings; however, this is hardly the "idea" that we have of a healing service! It's so important that we hear His voice and not do things our way, but that we be docile to the Holy Spirit and give Him the freedom to call the shots. Jesus said that His sheep "know His voice" (John 10:4). Is He your shepherd?

# STAND ON HIS WORD!

"Put on the whole armor of God, that you may be able to stand against the wiles of the devil" (Ephesians 6:11).

The Lord has provided us with a spiritual armor so that we may be able to stand on the solid foundation of His Word, which is the only solid foundation there is against the enemy. The Word of God is the only true reality and as we respond and obey the Word, we stand. James says:

"But be doers of the Word, and not hearers only, deceiving yourselves" (James 1:22).

Therefore, if we are ignorant of the Scriptures, we will not be able to stand. We will believe the enemy's lies and fall for the negative report. We will not be able to walk by faith. We will waver. Our minds, emotions or circumstances will rule us, rather than the Holy Spirit. Putting on the whole armor of God is really a response of faith and obedience to the Word of God.

When Joseph and Mary took the baby Jesus to be presented at the temple, there was one "righteous and devout" believer named Simeon who had been waiting for the "consolation of Israel." (Luke 2:25) The Lord had promised him that he would not die without seeing the promised Messiah. So as Joseph and Mary were bringing Jesus to the temple, the Holy Spirit led Simeon into the temple. Talk about the perfect timing of the Holy Spirit! "And inspired by the Spirit he came into the temple; and when the parents brought in the child Jesus, to do for Him according to the custom of the law, he took Him up in his arms and blessed God and said, Lord, now lettest thou thy servant depart in peace, ACCORDING TO THY WORD, for mine eyes have seen thy salvation..."(Luke 2:27-30). Throughout all those years of waiting Simeon stood on God's Word, His promise, believing that "any day now" he would see the Messiah.

"Our soul waits for the Lord; He is our help and shield.

Yea, our heart is glad in Him, because we trust in His holy name." (Ps. 33:20-21).

I believe that at that time there were a lot of temple members, but very few believers. I imagine the situation was much like today; God's people distracted (maybe even with Church activity!), discouraged or in love with the world. Sometimes the toughest thing is to stand on the promise and believe that it will come to pass, no matter what the circumstances tell us. It's at this time of "waiting" that the enemy, that liar and "father of all lies" (John 8:44) comes to attack our minds with doubts, deception, distraction and discouragement . Watch out for the 4 d's, they come from the pit of hell!

Only two people in the entire Jerusalem area were shown the Messiah! Those who believed, who were waiting, saw the promise! They had the "BELT OF TRUTH" (Ephesians 6:14) girding their loins which enabled them to remain focused on the truth of the promise of the Messiah and not get distracted as they waited for Him. The other person who saw the Messiah was the prophetess Anna. "She did not depart from the temple, worshipping with fasting and prayer night and day. And coming up at that very hour she gave thanks to God...." (Luke2:37-38). This Anna was quite a lady; she did not depart from the temple; she worshipped, fasted and prayed NIGHT AND DAY! Do you think she was "focused?" No wander Jesus says in Matthew ll:12 that the "kingdom of heaven has suffered violence, and men of violence take it by force." The Lord is looking for a few "spiritually violent" people today! This business about following Jesus and getting into the "promised life" is not for double-minded, wishy-washy, lukewarm people! It takes everything we've got! Simeon and Anna were able to stand in the truth, knowing that "God is not man, that He should lie, or a son of man, that he should repent, Has He said, and will He not do it? Or has He spoken, and will he not fulfill it? (Numbers 23:19).

Imagine Joshua and Caleb going around in circles for forty years, unable to enter the Promised Land, because of others' unbelief! For forty years they believed and trusted God that the promise would still be there for them after the forty year "delay."

"For ever, O Lord, thy word is firmly fixed in the heavens."
(Ps. 119:89)

The Word of God is not like the stock market! Forever it is fixed,
settled; if God said it, that settles it. They saw their generation die
in the desert until they were the only two left. That "SHIELD OF
FAITH" (Ephesians 6:16) helped them stay standing and believing
God's promises in spite of the "flaming darts of the evil one" of
lies, doubts and discouragement. After the 40-year delay they did
not allow their "age" nor their "health" to keep them from taking
over what God had promised them. Caleb said:

> "....I am this day 85 years old. I am still as strong to this
> day as I was in the day that Moses sent me; my strength
> now is as my strength was then, for war, and for going and
> coming. So now give me this hill country...." (Joshua
> 14:11-12)

I like that. No trace of discouragement, weariness, bitterness,
anger, resentment. He was ready! Not ready for retirement, but
ready for taking over some mountains and killing some giants!
Just before Joshua died he told the Israelites: "...not one thing has
failed of all the good things which the Lord your God promised
concerning you; all have come to pass for you, not one of them has
failed." (Joshua 23:14) Isn't this powerful? He was able to take
a panoramic view of God's dealings with His people and was able
to say "everything the Lord promised has come to pass!" Their
faith in God and His Word shielded them from the lies, deception
and negativity from the enemy!
The Virgin Mary had on her feet "THE EQUIPMENT OF THE
GOSPEL OF PEACE" (Ephesians 6:15; Luke1:39) when she "arose
and went with haste into the hill country" to visit her cousin Elizabeth. She was ready and willing to walk 90 miles by herself to take
the good news of Jesus the Messiah to her cousin. Proclaiming the
good news of salvation, the fact that there is reconciliation with God
available to sinful humanity through the blood of Jesus, is part of
the armor of God. If you are not proclaiming the Gospel, your feet

are not protected! It's hard to stand with hurt feet! Mary had that readiness and willingness to GO! Do you? There are NO excuses! It's God's command! (Mark 16:15) Recently I was at an airport waiting for a flight to take me back home. There was a young man near me acting in a very obnoxious way. As we were boarding, I told the Lord "Please don't let him sit by me. I'm tired; I don't want to be bothered by anyone; I don't feel like talking to anyone." Guess who sat next to me? That same young man! I didn't have to walk 90 miles, I just had to overcome myself! But God is gracious, and He made it easy for me to share the Gospel with the young man. He's looking for our willingness! My dear brothers and sisters, we have been "strategically" placed in our families, neighborhoods, workplaces, cities and nations to reach certain people that only we can reach. They are our assignments! The Lord is counting on us to bring that harvest in! When the Holy Spirit was released in our lives, we received power to be His witnesses (Acts 1:8). Use that Power! Put your shoes on! The Holy Spirit is released as soon as you start sharing the Gospel!

Peter put the "BREASTPLATE OF RIGHTEOUSNESS" (Ephesians 6:14) firmly in place when he was asked to go to the home of Cornelius, a gentile Roman centurion. Good Jewish boys did not contaminate themselves by entering the home of a heathen! That was unheard of! The Lord had to speak to him through a vision three times, and when Cornelius' men went to fetch him the Spirit told Peter "Behold, three men are looking for you. Rise and go down, and accompany them without hesitation; for I have sent them." (Acts 10:19-20) The Apostle Paul says in 1 Thessalonians 5:8 that this breastplate is "of faith and love." This is what Peter was exercising, and through his ministry at Cornelius' house "the gift of the Holy Spirit" was poured out on the Gentiles, fulfilling God's command of preaching the Gospel to every creature, "for they heard them speaking in tongues and extolling God." (Acts 10:45-56) Afterwards in Jerusalem "the circumcision party criticized him, saying, Why did you go to uncircumcised men and eat with them?" (Acts 11:3) After Peter explained to them what had happened, "…they were silenced. And they glorified God, saying, 'Then to the Gentiles also God has granted repentance unto life'." (v. 18)

Sometimes obeying the voice of the Lord will not be understood nor approved by those around you, even by those that love you the most! But it's the Lord the One we have to obey! In Acts 4, after the miraculous healing of the crippled man, the religious authorities warned Peter and John "not to speak or teach at all in the name of Jesus." (v.18) This is how they responded to their threats: "But Peter and John answered them, 'Whether it is right in the sight of God to listen to you rather than to God, you must judge; for we cannot but speak of what we have seen and heard'." (v.19-20)

In the letter to the Philippians, Paul says that he didn't have a righteousness of his own, based on law, "but that which is through faith in Christ, the righteousness from God that depends on faith…" (3:9).

This righteousness is a gift from God, not from works, and is received through faith in Jesus Christ. This is the breastplate that guards our hearts. What a gift! Peter had to know in his heart that this "righteousness" was not from himself; it didn't come from what he did or did not do, but rather it came through faith in Jesus Christ. Later on, in the letter to the Galatians, we see that Peter somehow got intimidated by the circumcision party and Paul had to confront him because he "was not straightforward about the truth of the Gospel" (Galatians 2:14). This is a lesson for every believer! We must know in our hearts that this righteousness comes from God and not from ourselves, "because by works of the law shall no one be justified"(16); all of us have sinned and fallen short of the glory of God (Romans 3:23). This good news cannot be compromised! It's through the Blood of Jesus that we have been redeemed and our sins forgiven (Ephesians 1:7) and received right standing before God (Romans 5:9)! We receive God's righteousness "through faith in Jesus Christ for all who believe" (Romans 3:22). Guard your heart with that truth!

The disciple Ananias made sure his "HELMET OF SALVA-TION" (Ephesians 6:17) was guarding his mind as he obeyed the voice of the Lord (Acts 9:10-17). Imagine, the Lord tells him to go and lay hands on Saul of Tarsus (for prayer, not for strangling him!), the greatest persecutor and enemy of the Church at the time. Ananias couldn't believe it! He was afraid! He told the Lord:

"Lord, I have heard from many about this man, how much evil he has done to thy saints in Jerusalem; and here he has authority from the chief priests to bind all who call upon thy name." The Lord had to reassure him that he had heard correctly.

> "Go, for he is a chosen instrument of mine to carry my name before the Gentiles and kings...."

So Ananias went! How important to hear the voice of the Lord so that His plans and purposes are carried out! How important to obey when we hear His voice! Ananias, a disciple, had made himself available to be used by God. He literally brought sight to Saul as he laid his hands on him, for "something like scales fell from his eyes." (v.18). The Lord used Ananias to launch Saul into his calling. Ananias brought vision and mission! The Bible says that "in the synagogues immediately he (Paul) proclaimed Jesus, saying, He is the Son of God." (Acts 9:20). Our minds need protection because this is the area of the battlefield and the enemy will come with a "better plan" to try to stop us. If not, he will try to sow fear in us so that we don't do what we're supposed to do. The enemy will always try to thwart the Lord's plan. We need to discern which voice we're hearing: the Holy Spirit's, our own, or the devil's. That's why we must "take every thought captive to obey Christ" (2 Corinthians 10:5). Once we know it's the Lord's voice, we stand, and the helmet will do its work of protecting our minds.

We look to Jesus to learn how to use "The SWORD OF THE SPIRIT" effectively (Ephesians 6:17). The sword of the Spirit is the Word of God; it is the rhema Word, which is the Word quickened by the Holy Spirit. The Word of God and the Holy Spirit are a team! They work together. In Matthew 4:1-11 we see how "Jesus was led up by the Spirit into the wilderness to be tempted by the devil" (v.1). The "attacks" or temptations from the enemy came in the form of words. Three times Jesus took His "sword" out to come against the enemy. Jesus said "For it is written" three times (v.4,7,10) as He stood on the Word of God to defend Himself. Satan, who is a murderer and a liar (John 8:44), comes to "steal, kill, and destroy"

(John 10:10). Jesus is "the Truth" and "the Life" (John 14:6) and "appeared to destroy the works of the devil" (1John 3:8). The lies of the enemy are fought with the Truth, the Word of God, not with the wisdom from the world! Let me share a story with you. On my first trip to Uganda we encountered a young lady who had an animal spirit; she barked like a dog and made all the dog "noises" that dogs make. She could not hold a conversation. She acted like a dog. Her mother was into witchcraft. She was ministered to and by the time we left she could say a few words. I just saw her again (two years later), totally set free and glowing with the love of Jesus. It was the power of the Holy Spirit, using the "sword of the Spirit" that set this captive free! In America she would have been diagnosed as schizophrenic and placed in a mental institution! We have to believe that "the weapons of our warfare are not worldly but have divine power to destroy strongholds!" (2 Corinthians 10:4)

Not only did Jesus defeat the devil in the wilderness, but Jesus triumphed over the devil in the Cross (Colossians 2:15)! Now it is up to us to believe and walk into that victory; we must learn to enforce it. How do we overcome the enemy in our daily lives? By the power of the Holy Spirit and the Word of God. Let's look at Jesus, our model. He was submitted to the Father. He lived a life of obedience. Jesus said "...the Son can do nothing of his own accord, but only what he sees the Father doing; for whatever he does, that the Son does likewise" (John 5:19). James 4:7 says:

"Submit yourselves therefore to God.
Resist the devil and he will flee from you."

The first thing we have to be is submitted to the Lord. This means living a life of obedience to the Lord, in accord with His Word; then we can resist the devil using the Sword of the Spirit just like Jesus. Then we can be assured that the devil will flee. I was on my way to the island of Malta to preach, and I had a three-hour wait in the London airport. My mother had recently had a triple bypass; I had asked the Lord for guidance and clearly He had given me the go-ahead for Malta. As I waited in the airport, the enemy started to torment me with his lies, telling me that "I shouldn't have taken this trip; that when I would get to Malta I would find that mom was dead, and I would have to go back home. Take a plane back home now, instead of the one to Malta." Right there in my seat I opened my mouth and started to rebuke the enemy, using the Word of God. It went something like this: "devil, get out of my life now, in the name of Jesus. He who is in me is greater than you who are in the world. The Lord has sent me to proclaim the Gospel to every creature; I will go to Malta and preach the Gospel; people will be saved, healed and restored. I'm on assignment. I have you under my feet. I command every tormenting spirit, every lying spirit to leave me now. Thank you, Jesus for your victory. I speak healing to my mom now; she will not die, but live." I did not waver from this position and started to use my gift of tongues. I went to Malta, came back home, and mom was alive and kicking. Thank you, Jesus!

During this time of waiting the enemy will come to try to prevent you from entering into your "destiny." The enemy will try to blur your vision with lies and doubts. The Lord has allowed these "attacks" to come against you in order to train you and mature you. It's a time of perseverance and pressing in, of not giving up. It's a time to stay focused and not distracted nor discouraged. It's a testing and refining of your faith. (1 Peter 1:6-7) Here's the problem I see with a lot of people: they don't know the Word of God; therefore they don't have much truth inside of them. They don't have swords! How can you fight the lies of the enemy without the Sword of the Spirit?

How much do you want God and His plan for your life? Paul says in Philippians 3:13-14

"...I've got my eye on the goal, where God is beckoning us onward—to Jesus. I'm off and running, and I'm not turning back. So let's keep focused on that goal, Those of us who want everything God has for us." (*The Message, The Bible in Contemporary Language*).

Remember, to fight the lies of the enemy we do it with the truth of the Word of God, as the Holy Spirit quickens the Word. Will you make an effort to study the Bible on a daily basis?

# KEEP STANDING!

"Therefore take the whole armor of God, that you may be able to withstand in the evil day, and having done all, to stand" (Ephesians 6:13).

Don't take the armor off, because "…Your adversary the devil prowls around like a roaring lion, seeking someone to devour"(1 Peter 5:8). Don't you be that "someone!"

It's interesting to see that when the promise draws near, when victory is around the corner, the enemy comes to attack big time. So don't let your guard down; don't fall asleep! The enemy wants us to think he's a roaring lion, but he really is a toothless dog! Jesus is the Lion of the Tribe of Judah! Have you ever thought how dark and dreary that dungeon must have been for Joseph just before his promotion? (Genesis 41:14;41)

The Israelites spent 40 years in the wilderness before entering into the Promised Land and while they:

"dwelt in Shittim the people began to play the harlot with the daughters of Moab. These invited the people to the sacrifices of their gods, and the people ate, and bowed down to their gods." (Numbers 25:1-2)

Now, Shittim was a site in Moab, east of the Jordan River and opposite Jericho. In a sense, they could "see" the promise; it was just a river away! It was here that the Moabites seduced the Israelites into apostasy! Just before entering the Promised Land! It was a demonic strategy that came from "the counsel of Balaam" (Numbers 31:16), a false prophet who had been hired by Balak, the king of the Moabites, to curse the Israelites (Numbers 22-23). The curses didn't work because God's protection was upon His people. However, the enemy came up with another strategy against God's people so that God would not bless His people. The strategy was to seduce the Israelites into idolatry through sexual immorality. That's exactly what happened; the sin was punished and dealt with—the offenders were hanged! (Numbers 25:4), but the Lord in His mercy and faithfulness did not withdraw His promise to enter His people into the Promised Land. What I'm trying to show you is that the enemy will attack and try to tempt you out of God's will for your life just before the breakthrough. Some people give up and never enter into their destiny.

As you know, the Israelites were in bondage in Egypt for over 400 years; but there was a promise of deliverance and a new life in the Promised Land. However, things got really bad for them before the Exodus. Pharaoh placed hard taskmasters over them to "afflict them with heavy burdens" and "made their lives bitter with hard service…" (Exodus 1:11;14). Just before the birth of Moses, their deliverer, Pharaoh gave the command to kill every Hebrew male baby (Exodus 1:22). Stephen says in Acts 7:17-20:

"But as the time of the promise drew near, which God had granted to Abraham, the people grew and multiplied in Egypt till there arose over Egypt another king who had not known Joseph. He dealt craftily with our race and forced our fathers to expose their infants, that they might not be kept alive. At this time Moses was born, and was beautiful before God."

The enemy comes to attack as the promise draws near, so this is not the time for us to draw back! Instead, "Draw near to God and He will draw near to you." (James 4:8) I like how THE MESSAGE, The Bible in Contemporary Language, interprets Hebrews 10:36-39:

"But you need to stick it out, staying with God's plan so you'll be there for the promised completion. It won't be long now, He's on the way; He'll show up most any minute. But anyone who is right with Me thrives on loyal trust; if he cuts and runs, I won't be very happy. But we're not quitters who lose out. Oh, no! We'll stay with it and survive, trusting all the way."

Don't quit!

# STEP OVER THE ENEMY!

"You shall tread upon the lion and the cobra, the young lion and the serpent you shall trample underfoot." Ps. 91:13

Do you know where your enemies belong? Under your feet! Now, your enemies are not human beings, but the unseen spiritual forces of wickedness released against us (Ephesians 6:12); things such as fear, depression, hopelessness, negativity, anxiety, discouragement, oppression, sickness and disease, deception and the like. Jesus triumphed at the Cross over the enemy (Colossians2:14-15) and now is seated at God's:

> "right hand in the heavenly places, far above all rule and authority and power and dominion and above every name that is named, not only in this age but also in that which is to come, and He has put all things under His feet and has made Him the head over all things..." (Ephesians 1:20-22).

This is really good news! Everything that has a name belongs under the feet of Jesus! So what is the name of your problem? It's under the feet of Jesus! Now, there's even more good news for us! Ephesians 2:6 says that we have been raised up with him and that He has:

> "made us sit with Him in the heavenly places in Christ Jesus...."

In other words, our enemies are under our feet also, because now we are seated with Christ and He is seated at the highest place! We are not "under the circumstances," but above them! It's important to know that when we stand in intercession before the throne we're doing it from a place of authority. The enemy has been defeated at the Cross and we are enforcing Jesus' victory over the enemy. We are to rise up and start stepping over our enemies. Jesus told His disciples in Luke 10:19:

"Behold, I have given you authority to tread
upon serpents and scorpions and over all the
power of the enemy; and nothing shall hurt you."

As Joshua and the Israelites started to take over the promised
land, Joshua told the Israelite captains in Joshua 10:24(b) "Come
near, put your feet upon the necks of these (enemy) kings."

It's time for us to stop talking, gossiping, grumbling and complaining and start stepping over our real enemies! And as we do,
we are fulfilling part of the Church's commission, which is to make
His enemies His footstool. (Ps. 110:1) The writer of Hebrews says
that after Jesus:

"sat down at the right hand of God, from that time waiting
till His enemies are made His footstool." (10:12-13)
(NKJ)

Unless we understand this, we will always be "under the circumstances" and will walk in defeat. God's purpose for us is that
we exercise our authority in Christ and start stepping and treading
over our enemies! You have to quit looking at yourself as a victim
and start looking at yourself as "more than a conqueror through Him
who loved us." (Romans 8:37) Understand that God has already
cursed the enemy: "...upon your belly you shall go, and dust you
shall eat all the days of your life." (Genesis 3:14) The Psalmist
in Psalm 72: 9 says "May His foes bow down before Him, and His
enemies lick the dust!" King David says in Ps. 18:37-38:

"I pursued my enemies and overtook them;
and did not turn back till they were consumed.
I thrust them through, so that they were not able
to rise; they fell under my feet."

Our enemies are to be kept under our feet! In other words,
we crush them and keep them bound because "He who is in you

is greater than he who is in the world." (1 John 4:4) This is part of our inheritance as children of God! Start taking authority and stepping over your enemies in small ways, so that when you are faced with a big crisis or difficulty you know what to do right away. I remember when I first started going to the women's jail every Saturday morning, that on Friday nights everything that could go wrong went wrong. My son Eddy broke his collarbone playing football on a Friday; I spent the night nursing him. My son Victor cut his foot on a Friday night; if the toilet overflowed it was on a Friday night and if any of my children broke their curfews, it would be on a Friday night. It was as though a spirit of confusion would come against the family. I was so discouraged at one point that I almost quit the jail ministry, until the Lord showed me that these were attacks from the enemy and that I should start exercising my authority over him. The Lord reminded me of the Apostle Paul and how he persevered through every trial and tribulation (2 Corinthians 11:23-28). I started to step over the enemy (Luke 10:19) and the circumstances started to change. The house situation got in control and then the enemy started to attack my body on Friday nights as I slept, with sharp pains in my back. I learned to take authority over that as well and for ten years I have been going to the women's jail. Many times in our homes the children "suddenly" start to fight and argue; rise up and step and trample over that spirit of strife and division (not over your kids!). Command it out of your house in the name of Jesus! Paul says in Romans 16:20:

"the God of peace will soon crush Satan under your feet."

When we walk in the peace of God we crush the enemy under our feet. He keeps us in "perfect peace" (Isaiah 26:3) as we trust in Him; so don't lose your peace because that's really how we crush the enemy! You can stay cool, calm and collected by the power of His Holy Spirit, even in very difficult situations! When we lose our peace, we think and say crazy things, maybe even act them out! We don't give God a chance to move! That's why the Apostle Paul says:

"Have no anxiety about anything, but in everything by prayer and supplication with thanksgiving let your requests be made known to God. And the PEACE OF GOD, which passes all understanding, will keep your hearts and your minds in Christ Jesus." (Philippians 4:6-7)

Remember that you are seated in heavenly places with Christ Jesus and that the enemy belongs under your feet, not over your head! We are under the Lordship of Jesus Christ not under the rule of an enemy king! Remember that:

"God has highly exalted Him (Jesus) and bestowed on him
the name which is above every name, that at the name of Jesus every knee should bow, in heaven and on earth and under the earth..." (Philippians 2:9-10) our enemies included!

Cora, an inmate at the Women's Detention Center, was very downcast and depressed. She would come to the Bible class looking like the "walking dead." I was teaching the women about spiritual warfare and how they needed to take authority over the enemy who comes "to steal, kill and destroy" everything in their lives (John 10:10). One day Cora said to me "Sister Maria, could you pray for me so that this depression leaves me?" I told her that I would not pray for her, that I had been teaching them how to pray for themselves. I said "Cora, I can pray for you and you'll be okay for a day or so. But I want you to learn to pray for yourself so that you can keep your deliverance. I come to the jail once a week; what are you going to do the rest of the week?" Cora got up and started to confess her faith in Christ Jesus and what He had accomplished on the Cross for her; she took authority over her enemy, depression, and started to step over it with her feet and commanded it to leave her in the name of Jesus. She asked the Holy Spirit to fill her with joy and she started to sing. It was amazing to watch the transformation in Cora's face as she sang to the Lord. She started to laugh as the depression left. Since that day the first one to show up in Bible class was Cora; she came joyfully and just wanted to help us in any way she could. When she went to court, the Lord gave her a miracle. Her time in jail was cut to less than half the time and she left early to her native land. From there she wrote saying she had found a church and had been baptized. Cora had learned to walk in the power of the Holy Spirit and to "step" over her enemies. Thank you, Jesus!

Look at this powerful promise from Isaiah 49:23:

"Kings shall be your foster fathers, and their queens your nursing mothers, with their faces to the ground they shall bow down to you, and lick the dust of your feet. Then you will know that I am the Lord; those who wait for me shall not be put to shame."

# YOU'RE WALKING THROUGH!

"Even though I walk though the valley of the shadow of death, I fear no evil; for thou art with me; thy rod and thy staff, they comfort me." (Psalm 23:4)

Whatever we are going through, we are just going through it. We don't want to remain "stuck." As Psalm 23 says, He is with us, leading us through. It's not the last chapter in your life! You must believe this. Years ago when I went "through" financial disaster and "through" the breakup of my marriage, most people looked at me with great pity, as if my life were over. It was a very difficult time for me, but my life was far from over. All I knew was that Jesus was with me and walking me through, and what the devil had intended for harm the Lord would change around for my good and His glory! His report for my life, according to Jeremiah, was that He had:

"plans for welfare and not for evil, to give me a future and a hope." (Jeremiah 29:11)

I chose to believe this and to continue to allow Him to walk me "through." Whatever you're going through, it will lead somewhere. God is in it. Ps. 84 calls those roads the "highways to Zion."

"Blessed are the men whose strength is in Thee,
in whose hearts are the highways to Zion.
As they go through the valley of Baca
They make it a place of springs...." (Psalm 84:3-4)

As we thank and praise the Lord in every valley we go through, they will become a "place of springs" to refresh and strengthen us in our journey. (Numbers 21:16-18)

The Lord is the "Lord of the Breakthrough." In 2 Samuel 5:20 David experiences victory over his enemies and he said "The Lord has broken through my enemies...." Isn't He the one that "shatters the doors of bronze, and cuts in two the bars of iron?" (Psalm 107:16) No matter how hard is the situation facing you, the Lord will break through on to victory. He can do all things but fail.

> "He who opens the breach will go up before them; they will break through and pass the gate, going out by it. Their king will pass on before them, the Lord at their head." (Micah 2:13)

As King David left Jerusalem escaping from his own son Absalom, who had led a coup d'etat (2 Samuel 15:13-16), King David was heartbroken. Imagine the pain of being illegally kicked out from his throne, and by his own son. What betrayal! What self-seeking and ambition! Now look as to how the Lord ministered to him and his men as he "passed a little beyond the summit" (2 Samuel 16). Somebody came to meet him with:

> "a couple of asses saddled, bearing two hundred loaves of bread, a hundred bunches of raisins, a hundred of summer fruits, and a skin of wine." (v.1)

King David asked the man "Why have you brought these? Ziba answered, the asses are for the king's household to ride on, the bread and summer fruit for the young men to eat, and the wine for those who faint in the wilderness to drink." The Lord will always provide for our needs as we are walking through; He will provide us with "donkeys" to get us through: people who will come to us just at the right time and the right place. I remember often how my sister and brother-in-law would "drop by" at just the right time, and many times he would say "I'll take you to the grocery store so that you can fill up the refrigerator," not knowing that I really needed to do just that but had no money! Thank you, Jesus!

The Lord has already provided for our sustenance: the bread, raisins and summer fruit that strengthen us as we walk through. Jesus said that:

> "Man shall not live by bread alone, but by every word that

proceeds from the mouth of God." (Matthew 4:4)

The Word of God has quickening power to raise us up. Just like the Israelites in the desert, we have to gather every morning the "manna" of His Word, His own special Word that He speaks to us personally. As Catholics we have the Eucharist, the real presence of Jesus in the Bread that graces, strengthens and heals us from moment to moment as we receive Him in faith. We also have the "wine" of the Holy Spirit to gladden us and fill us with joy, because the "joy of the Lord is our strength." (Nehemiah 8:10) We don't need to go to "Happy Hour" at the local bar! Just like the day of Pentecost, the Holy Spirit Himself fills us with the joy of Jesus, who was "anointed with the oil of gladness" like no one else (Hebrews 1:9). Amen!

There is a great promise for us in Isaiah 43:1-2 of His faithfulness to us as we "go through" difficulties:

"Fear not, for I have redeemed you; I have called you by name, you are mine. When you pass through the waters I will be with you; and through the rivers, they shall not overwhelm you; when you walk through fire you shall not be burned, and the flame shall not consume you."

The Lord is telling us that no matter what we go through He will see us "through!" No matter what we're going through we should not fear because He is with us! We will not be "drowned" by our problems nor "burned" by them! I know that the Lord always provides for a way out, even if it's a close call! The two Israelite spies sent into Jericho had to be let "down by a rope through the window" by Rahab for them to escape into safety (Joshua 2:15). David escaped from Saul's men who wanted to kill him; "So Michael let David down through the window; and he fled away and escaped." (1 Samuel 19:12) After Paul's conversion the religious leaders in Jerusalem wanted to kill him "but his disciples took him by night and let him down over the wall, lowering him in a basket" (Acts 9:25). No matter how tough the situation the Lord is in control and He provides a way out and people to help us get "through." Just make sure that you go "down," that you "humble yourself therefore under the mighty hand of God, that in due time he may exalt you." (1 Peter 5:6) In other words, we must go "down" before we can go up. The two spies, David and Paul, had a close call but the Lord prevailed. They did not freak out, grumble or complain but simply went "through" the way out provided by the Lord. They saw the hand of God in an extremely difficult situation and held on to Him. This is His promise:

> "Every test that you have experienced is the kind that normally comes to people. But God keeps His promise, and He will not allow you to be beyond your power to remain firm; at the time you are put to the test, He will give you the strength to endure it, and so provide you with a way out." (1 Corinthians 10:13 New Testament, Today's English Version)

My dear brothers and sisters, no situation is harder than a hardened human heart. If today you're walking with Him, you have already tasted His power and grace in changing your life around by bringing you to Jesus. He has a plan for your life. He will not abandon His children (Ps 27:10). Now He calls us to trust Him and to walk by faith. Romans 8:32 says:

> "He who did not spare His own Son but gave Him up for us all, will he not also give us all things with Him?"

He will give us "all things" in this journey into our "destiny" as we walk by faith.

As we "go through" difficulties and trials, we can count on the Lord's protection, provision, power, presence, peace and purpose. I call them the 6 p's.

Protection: Isaiah 43:1-2 "Fear not, for I have redeemed you; I have called you by name, you are mine. When you pass through the waters I will be with you; and through the rivers, they shall not overwhelm you; when you walk through the fire you shall not be burned and the flame shall not consume you."

Provision: Ps. 66:12 "...we went through fire and through water; yet thou hast brought us forth to a spacious place."

Power: Ps. 78:13 "He divided the sea and let them pass through it, and made the waters stand like a heap."

Presence: Exodus 33:14 "And He said, My Presence will go with you, and I will give you rest."

Peace: Isaiah 26:3 "Thou dost keep him in perfect peace, whose mind is stayed on thee, because he trusts in Thee."

Purpose: Ps. 138:8 "The Lord will fulfill His purpose for me; thy steadfast love, O Lord, endures forever. Do not forsake the work of thy hands."

Whatever you're going through, like David, we believe and say:

"Though I walk in the midst of trouble, thou dost preserve my life; thou dost stretch out thy hand against the wrath of my enemies, and thy right hand delivers me." (Ps. 138:7)

Like the Apostle Paul we can declare that:

"The Lord will rescue me from every evil and save me for His heavenly kingdom..." 2 Timothy 4:18.

Like the prophet Nahum (1:7) we proclaim that:

"The Lord is good, a stronghold in the day of trouble; He knows those who take refuge in Him."

Like the prophet Jeremiah in chapter 20:11, trust that:

"the Lord is with me as a dread warrior; therefore my persecutors will stumble, they will not overcome me. They will be greatly shamed for they will not succeed. Their eternal dishonor will never be forgotten."

Whatever you are going through, He's with you! This is not the last chapter in your journey!

"Remember not the former things, nor consider the things of old. Behold, I am doing a new thing; now it springs forth, do you not perceive it? I will make a way in the wilderness and rivers in the desert." (Isaiah 43:18-19)

# STRENGHTEN YOURSELF IN THE LORD!

"But David strengthened himself in the Lord His God" (1Samuel 30:6b).

There are times in our lives when we have to encourage and strengthen ourselves; we must learn how to strengthen ourselves in God. Everything that could go wrong has gone wrong. There's no prayer group that day, your prayer partner is out of town, no Bible class and it's just you and God and you're having a rotten day. I believe that finding yourself "alone" is the Lord's doing, so that you turn to Him completely, like King Hezekiah, who "turned his face toward the wall, and prayed to the Lord...." (Isaiah 38:2) Remember, He's interested in the journey into your destiny; He's looking at your heart! 2 Chronicles 16:9 says:

"The eyes of the Lord roam over the whole earth, to encourage those who are devoted to Him wholeheartedly." (NAB)

Ps. 46: 1 says:

"God is our refuge and strength, a very present help in trouble."

The Lord is the Lord of "now"; He is Lord over your circumstances; our help comes from Him! He is "a very present help!" He's at the right hand of God making intercession for us (Romans 8:34). " For all the promises of God in Him are Yes, and in Him Amen...." (2 Corinthians 1:20) He's given us His Holy Spirit to be with us always. Ps. 121:3-4 says:

"He will not let your foot be moved,
He who keeps you will not slumber.
Behold, He who keeps Israel
Will neither slumber nor sleep." Amen!
David in 1 Samuel 30 is going through a very, very difficult

time. He's living in exile in Ziklag, in the land of the Philistines, because he's afraid of getting killed by King Saul. The Philistines have rejected his help in a battle against the Israelites, and when he and his men return to Ziklag,

> "they found it burned with fire, and their wives and sons and daughters taken captive. Then David and the people who were with him raised their voices and wept, until they had no more strength to weep." (v.3-4)

Have you ever wept to the point of exhaustion, that you have no strength left to weep? I have, and at that moment it's God and you. I wept so much that my face was deformed. I had made a huge mistake of signing a legal document that I never should have signed! But I turned to the Lord and in faith started thanking and praising Him. He changed "my mourning into dancing!" (Ps.30:11) He is true to His Word!

> "Weeping may endure for the night,
> but joy comes in the morning." (Ps. 30:5) (NKJ)

I told the Lord "I need a word from you, Papa." Before going to sleep my sister prayed that the Lord would speak to me during the night, and He did. He said "Worship Me in the delay." That's all that I needed at that moment: to hear His voice. It gave me much comfort and encouragement.

The situation for David worsened, "for the people spoke of stoning him, because all the people were bitter in soul..." and David was greatly distressed. "But David strengthened himself in the Lord His God." (v.6) Not only did the enemy come to "steal, kill and destroy" (John 10:10), but now his own men had turned against him. A spirit of strife and division had definitely come into the group. Watch out when discouragement comes in! Stop it, because worse things will follow, as in this case. In previous times of desperation in David's life, Jonathan, David's friend, had sought David out and "strengthened his hand in God." (1 Samuel 23:16) But now David found himself alone, with his men turned against

him, with no Jonathan in sight. But we're never alone! The Lord
has promised to never leave us nor forsake us:

> "He is our refuge and strength, a very present help in
> trouble. Therefore we will not fear...." (Ps. 46:1-2)

In spite of all his troubles, David did not let fear control him. He
turned to the Lord for guidance; the Lord told him to:

> "Pursue, for you shall surely overtake and shall surely
> rescue." (v.8)

At times, we who are walking with the Lord, find ourselves "alone"
in our families. The enemy has come to steal, kill and destroy in our
homes, and he does it in different ways: addiction and alcoholism,
divorce and separation, depression, anorexia, sickness and disease,
pornography, strife and division, sexual immorality. Our homes
might look like "wastelands," but Jesus is with us, and by the power
of the Holy Spirit we can "destroy the works of the devil" (1 John
3:8). We can rescue and recover what the enemy has stolen from
us. "Greater is He that lives in me than he who is in the world" (1
John 4:4). Jesus and I are a majority! And His message is to take
authority over the enemy, in His name, and to tread over the "serpents and scorpions" that have invaded our homes. (Luke 10:19)
David pursued his enemies and:

> "... recovered all that the Amalekites had taken; and David
> rescued his two wives. Nothing was missing, whether small
> or great, sons or daughters, spoil or anything that had been
> taken; David brought back all." (1 Samuel 30:18-19)

We must know that if Jesus is the Lord of our lives, the kingdom of God is at hand, the kingdom is within us, and we have the
authority to kick the enemy out and recover what he has stolen.
The Lord says in Joel 2:24-25:

> "The threshing floors shall be full of grain, the vats shall

overflow with wine and oil. I will restore to you the years which the swarming locusts have eaten…."

The Lord also says in Isaiah 44:3:

"For I will pour water on the thirsty land, and streams on the dry ground; I will pour My Spirit on your descendants and My blessing on your offspring…."

So how do we encourage ourselves when we are faced with very difficult situations that seem to have no way out in the natural? How do we recover what the enemy has stolen?

1. Pray!

"Ask, and it will be given you; seek, and you will find; knock, and it will be opened to you. For everyone who asks receives, and he who seeks finds, and to him who knocks it will be opened. Or what man of you, if his son asks him for bread, will give him a stone? Or if he asks for a fish, will give him a serpent? If you then, who are evil, know how to give good gifts to your children, how much more will your Father who is in heaven give good things to those who ask Him!" (Matthew 7:7-11)

Are you waiting on God for a few good things? Then they're yours! He's the giver of every good and "perfect gift." (James 1:17) Talk to God about it; He doesn't suffer from mood swings. He's always the same, we can count on that. (Hebrews 13:8) "You do not have, because you do not ask" (James 4:2b). The Bible shows that Father Abraham lied and the Lord rescued him out of those messes. I had made the mistake of signing a legal document that I never should have signed. Therefore, as I talked to the Lord about it, and saw how faithful and true He was with Abraham, I was encouraged. I told the Lord "Signing this paper wasn't even a sin, Lord, I was just plain stupid! I need your help to get out of the mess I have placed myself in." Ps. 40:1-2 says:

"I waited patiently for the Lord;
He inclined to me and heard my cry.
He drew me up from the desolate pit,
out of the miry bog, and set my feet upon a rock...."

The Lord heard my cry and raised up a "deliverer" for me.
The husband of one of my sisters in the Lord, a lawyer, offered his
help! He said "I'll help you and I'll do my best, but Jesus will have
to fight this one." The Lord did fight for me as he used my friend
to get me out of the "pit"; eventually the settlement agreement I
had signed was set aside. Isn't it the heart of the Lord that there
be justice in the courts? Ps 37: 28 says:

"For the Lord loves justice; He will not forsake His
saints."

That's why David could say:

"Contend, O Lord, with those who contend with me;
fight against those who fight against me!
Take hold of shield and buckler,
And rise for my help!" (Ps. 35:1-2)

I believe that most of us limit the power of God in our lives.
Micah 7:7 says:

"But as for me, I will look to the Lord, I will wait for the
God of my salvation; my God will hear me."

It's very powerful when we pray the Word of God, which is His
will. The Apostle John says:

"And this is the confidence which we have in Him,
that if we ask anything according to His will
He hears us. And if we know that He hears us
in whatever we ask, we know that we have obtained

the requests made of him." (1 John 5:14-15)

What a promise! While in Nicaragua we were asked to pray for the successful heart surgery of a relative of the folks I was staying with. We prayed a very simple prayer, asking God that he wouldn't even need surgery. That's exactly what happened! Hands weren't even laid on him! Thank you, Jesus!

A friend and sister in the Lord had been diagnosed with a lump in her breast. She asked for prayer and when she went back to the doctor the lump was gone. After all, Jesus says to "heal every disease and every infirmity." (Matthew 10:1) We ask and He heals! Many people take the doctor's report as the final word and do not pray, therefore limiting the power of God in their lives.

Some situations require more prayer than others, but even then the Lord says:

"And will not God vindicate his elect, who cry to him day and night? Will He delay long over them? I tell you, He will vindicate them speedily...." (Luke 18:7-8)

My friend Suzy was very upset when her oldest son was kicked out of high school because of drug use. She didn't even know her son was using drugs! Suzy persevered years in prayer, never giving up; I admired how she never gave up believing that God would come through. Lamentations 3:25 says:

"The Lord is good to those who wait for Him, to the soul that seeks Him."

Her son was delivered from drug addiction, has graduated from the university, and now is thinking of entering into the priesthood! What the devil intends for destruction, Jesus turns around for our blessing and His glory, through the prayer of a "righteous" person! (James 5:16) If you have been washed clean with His blood, you have been made righteous (Romans 5:9) and have access to the throne of God! (Hebrews 4:16) Don't listen to the lies of the devil when he tells you that there's no use in praying and that your prayers will not amount to much, because the Word of God says just the opposite: that our prayer has "great power in its effects." (James 5:16) Like David in Ziklag, in moments when we are distressed and faced with discouragement and fear, let's turn to the Lord and not allow the circumstances nor our flesh control our decisions. The Holy Spirit, our Helper, our Comforter, the Spirit of truth and wisdom and revelation, will give us what we need. He will show us how to pray effectively. He is in us, the "rivers of living water" Jesus talked about in John 7:37-39. He is our sufficiency! (2 Cor. 12:9) When we are weak, then we are strong! Amen! His grace is sufficient!

I cannot adequately express the powerful effects of praying in tongues. Because this is such a powerful gift, the enemy has sown much confusion about it. Remember, every good gift comes from God. Everything that the Lord gives us is because we need it. Often, I don't know how to pray or how to focus my prayer; often, I don't know what is the root cause of the difficulty; often, I don't have the right words (either in Spanish or English!) and this is when the gift of tongues is really helpful. The Apostle Paul says in Romans 8:26:

"Likewise the Spirit helps us in our weakness;
for we do not know how to pray as we ought,
but the Spirit himself intercedes for us with sighs
too deep for words."

Can you grasp the power of what St. Paul is saying? Not only does the Spirit intercede for us, but He does it according to the will of God! Our prayers become like sharp arrows in the hand of God. They hit the "target." The Holy Spirit's intercession is His intervention. My 94-year-old uncle in Mexico had been bed-ridden and blind for quite a few years. My aunt, understandably so, was anxious and worried about him; so many times he had come close to death. She was afraid of being alone with him at the time of his departure from planet earth. I just prayed in tongues most of the time for this situation, knowing that the Holy Spirit was in control of everything. When my uncle passed away, he was not alone; he was surrounded by his wife and children and even the priest! What really impressed my aunt was that even the priest was there at the right moment. When we invite the Holy Spirit into the situation through the gift of tongues, He will intervene and will "do far more abundantly than all that we ask or think!" (Ephesians 3:20) Jesus will always be glorified through the Holy Spirit's intercession. In the letter of Jude, v.20, he says "But you, beloved, build yourselves up on your most holy faith; pray in the Holy Spirit." This means that when we pray in tongues, we strengthen ourselves; St. Paul says in 1 Cor. 14:4 "He who speaks in a tongue edifies Himself...." Do you see the relationship between being strong in the Spirit and praying in the Spirit? As we pray through in tongues as we wait on the Lord we can be assured that:

"they who wait for the Lord shall renew their strength,
they shall mount up with wings like eagles,
they shall run and not be weary,
they shall walk and not faint" (Isaiah 40:31).

What a promise! But this is not all! Tongues also refreshes us. In Isaiah 28:11-12 it says:

"...but by men of strange lips and with an alien tongue
the Lord will speak to this people, to whom He has said,
This is rest; give rest to the weary; and this is repose...."

There is strength and refreshment in the Spirit in our journey and we have access to this through the wonderful gift of tongues! Proverbs 5:15 says:

"Drink water from your own cistern, flowing water from your own well."

When we pray in tongues the "rivers of living water" (John 7:38-39) will start to flow in us and through us. There is a release of the Holy Spirit as we pray in tongues. Remember, the Holy Spirit is God; He is a person; He's the third person of the Trinity. It's in the Holy Spirit that our needs are met. In the Holy Spirit we find the power of God, health and healing, strength, renewing, wisdom, revelation, direction, joy. The other gifts of the Spirit will flow as needed, especially when we are ministering to others. Last year my mother was hemorrhaging to death on the fourth day after a triple bypass. She had lost four pints of blood and nurses were coming in and out of her room giving her blood transfusions, but she kept hemorrhaging. At this point I walked into her room, not knowing what was happening. I felt like weeping because mom was dying, but at that moment the "rivers of living water" started to rise in me and instead I obeyed the Word of God that says to "lay hands on the sick and they will recover" (Mark 16:18). I laid hands on mom and immediately started to pray in very loud tongues as the Spirit led. After I stopped praying I had a tremendous sense of peace. The nurses took mom to have a scan done (to see where the bleeding was coming from). The report: no more bleeding! It had stopped! It was a miraculous healing! The Holy Spirit intervened and told the hemorrhages to "STOP!"

Jesus told the Samaritan woman in John 4:14:

"...whoever drinks of the water that I shall give him will never thirst; the water that I shall give him will become in him a spring of water welling up to eternal life."

This is really important for us to understand, because "eternal life" is a quality of life; it is the "abundant life" that only Jesus can give, and we have continual access to this life as we "plug in" to the Spirit through the gift of tongues.

Another powerful reason to use the gift of tongues is to get access to the revelation knowledge of the Holy Spirit so that we can pray effectively. Jeremiah 33:3 says: "Call to me and I will answer you, and will tell you great and hidden things which you have not known." There are "hidden things" in our difficulties and trials that we cannot see with our natural eyes and when the Holy Spirit shows them to us we can respond appropriately to the information given. I was praying for a good friend of mine whose family was having financial difficulties. In the natural I couldn't understand why; they were both working and they were tithing. I prayed in tongues for this situation, and as I did, the Lord kept showing me their living room; specifically the Lord showed me a sculpture they had on a table. It was a figure of a depressed, poverty-stricken man carrying a sack of potatoes. I sensed the Lord telling me that they should get rid of it. I told my friend what I sensed the Lord had shown me, and she said that I was the second person that told her the same thing. She went ahead and threw the sculpture out of her house. The economic situation started to improve after this! Thank you, Jesus! God's ways are not our ways, are they? The important thing is to listen and obey!

Proverbs 8:34-45 says:

"Happy is the man who listens to me,
watching daily at my gates, waiting
beside my doors. For he who finds
me finds life and obtains favor from the Lord..."

2. Be Thankful!

"Enter His gates with thanksgiving...." (Psalm 100:4)

Thanksgiving is the key that opens the gates to be able to enter into His presence. It's the blood of Jesus that allows us to enter into His presence, but we enter with thanksgiving and praise. There is a protocol to enter into the presence of the Lord:

" Enter his courts with thanksgiving and His courts with praise" (Psalm100:4), not with grumbling and complaining! Needless to say, we need His presence and we need to learn how to enter in, especially during difficulties, when we don't feel much like giving thanks about anything! Why do we need His presence? First of all, it's in His presence that there is fullness of joy (Ps. 16:11). Why do we need His joy? Because the "joy of the Lord" is my strength! (Nehemiah 8:10)

His joy is the medicine that we need against depression and discouragement. It's in His presence that we are transformed and changed into His likeness (2 Cor. 3:18) and it's in that place of intimacy that He talks to us. Everything that we need is in His presence. "Let us come before His presence with thanksgiving." (Psalm 95:2)

Cultivate an attitude of gratitude during the "journey" into your destiny. The celebration of the Mass is a great opportunity to express our gratitude and thanksgiving to the Lord. The word Eucharist means "thanksgiving." The Apostle Paul writes in the letter to the Philippians 4:11-13:

"Not that I complain of want; for I have learned, in whatever state I am, to be content. I know how to be abased, and I know how to abound; in any and all circumstances I have learned the secret of facing plenty and hunger, abundance and want. I can do all things in Him who strengthens me."

I believe the Lord wants to impart this state of contentment as we journey into our "destiny."

The Apostle Paul tells us in Ephesians 5:18-20 to get filled with the Holy Spirit and then we will "always and for everything" give thanks in the name of our Lord Jesus Christ to God the Father." Is it possible to give thanks "always and for everything"? Is it possible to give thanks to the Lord for that person who has harmed you, for that situation that is causing you insomnia, for that rebellious child, and for that lawsuit that is pending? Only with the Holy Spirit can we do so! In our flesh we can't and we won't, but something happens when our precious Helper, the Holy Spirit, takes control of our lives. We start wanting to do those things that the Word of God says we must, instead of what we "feel like doing." It's just another lifestyle!

My friend Ana, 75 years old, slipped and fell when she was stepping out of the shower. She felt excruciating pain in her left hip, "more pain than in childbirth," as she describes it. In the midst of her pain, as she lay on the floor, she kept "thanking the Lord;" as she was being carried in the stretcher "she thanked the Lord" and as she waited for her doctor she kept "thanking the Lord." She literally thanked the Lord during this ordeal instead of grumbling and complaining. The result: the doctor was able to successfully place her hip bone back into the hip socket without any need for surgery; she had an amazing recovery; the nurses showed her kindness and compassion and she was surrounded by the presence of the Lord which gave her peace and comfort. Her "thanking the Lord' changed the atmosphere around her and the Holy Spirit acted on her behalf. In 1 Thessalonians 5:18 the Apostle Paul says to:

"give thanks in all circumstances; for this is the will of God in Christ Jesus for you."

A thankful heart is not only precious in the eyes of our God, but it is also a powerful weapon in His hand. Thanksgiving releases the miraculous in our lives so that our needs can be met, as was the case with my friend Ana (John 6:11; John 11:41; Jonah 2:9-10; 2Chronicles 20:21). I remind you that for the Apostle Paul thanksgiving was an important ingredient in his life.

"Continue steadfastly in prayer, being watchful in it with thanksgiving." (Colossians 4:2)

"Have no anxiety about anything, but in everything by prayer and supplication with thanksgiving let your requests be made known to God." (Phillipians 4:6)

"First of all, then, I urge that supplications, prayers, intercessions, and thanksgivings be made for all men...." (1 Timothy 2:1)

"And let the peace of Christ rule in your hearts, to which indeed you were called in the one body. And be thankful!" (Colossians 3:15)

"For everything created by God is good, and nothing is to be rejected if it is received with thanksgiving; for then it is consecrated by the word of God and prayer."
(1 Timothy 4:4-5)

"I do not cease to give thanks for you, remembering you in my prayers." (Ephesians 1:16)

"I give thanks to God always for you because of the grace of God which was given you in Christ Jesus...." (1 Corinthians 1:4)

"First, I thank my God through Jesus Christ for all of you, because your faith is proclaimed in all the world." (Romans 1:8)

"But thanks be to God, who in Christ always leads us in triumph." (2 Corinthians 2:14)

"We always thank God, the Father of our Lord Jesus Christ, when we pray for you, because we have heard of your faith in Christ Jesus and of the love which you have for all the saints." (Colossians 1:3-4).

"We give thanks to God always for you all, constantly mentioning you in our prayers, remembering before our God and Father your work of faith and labor of love...."
(1 Thessalonians 1:2-3)

"We are bound to give thanks to God always for you, brethren, as is fitting, because your faith is growing abundantly, and the love of every one of you for one another is increasing." (2 Thessalonians 1:3-4)

"I thank God whom I serve with a clear conscience...."
(2 Timothy 1:3)

According to Romans 1:21, not thanking God is one reason

why people become "futile in their thinking and their senseless minds [are] darkened." Not thanking God is one step in the wrong direction, away from His presence.

Will you now, start thanking the Lord in the midst of what you're going through?

3. Praise God!

"...and His courts with praise!" (Ps. 100:4)

Stop analyzing and start praising! When we're hit with adversity, difficulties and a long delay, it's easy to lose our focus, which is the Lord Jesus Christ, and to look at the circumstances. It's at this point that discouragement and self-pity may come in. That's exactly what we don't want to fall into. However, when we praise the Lord, we take our eyes off ourselves and the situation and instead we look at Him.

"My eyes are ever toward the Lord, for He will pluck my feet out of the net." (Ps. 25:15)

Praising the Lord causes us to look at Him, which in turn allows Him to us to take us out of the "net" of the enemy. As God's people, we're supposed to "walk by faith", not by sight (2 Cor. 5:7). We must operate in faith, because "without faith it is impossible to please God" (Hebrews 11:6). The Lord responds to faith! Ps. 22:3 says that the Lord is:

"enthroned on the praises of Israel."

That means that when we praise Him, He "shows up." And when He shows up He moves in power to comfort, heal, deliver and set free His people (Acts 16: 25-26). Usually when we're going through a tough time we grumble and complain; that's what's natural to us! Instead of the Holy Spirit being released, He is grieved! (Ephesians 4:30). On top of that, the enemy is attracted into our situation by the wrong use of our tongues. Recently, while in Nicaragua, I was teaching on praise and how we are to "continually offer up a sacrifice of praise to God..." (Hebrews 13:15) even when we don't "feel like it." One lady who owned a paint shop and had had no customers in the month of November decided that she would start praising the Lord inside her shop, rather than give in to hopelessness. She spent time praising God in Spanish and in tongues and her husband laughed at her. The next day she had three customers; just with the money from the sales of the first customer she had enough money to cover her bills for the month! Thank you, Jesus!

Praising the Lord was not invented by the Charismatic Renewal. It is the reason for our existence! It is God's way of pressing into His presence. Remember, His ways are not our ways (Isaiah 55:8)! We need to conform to His ways! 1 Peter 2:9 says:

> "But you are a chosen race, a royal priesthood,
> a holy nation, God's own people, that you may
> declare the wonderful deeds of him who called
> you out of darkness into his marvelous light."

That's exactly what we do when we praise the Lord: We declare His wonderful deeds! And we have so much to declare! In Luke 19, on Palm Sunday, as Jesus and the crowd were approaching Jerusalem, "the whole multitude of the disciples began to rejoice and praise God with a loud voice for all the mighty works that they had seen...." (v.37) I can just see them dancing, leaping and loudly praising the Lord!! However, some of the Pharisees in the crowd got upset and told Jesus "Teacher, rebuke your disciples. He answered, I tell you, if these were silent, the very stones would cry out." (v.39-40) The Pharisees refused to "rejoice and praise God" and they missed it! They ended up rejecting the Messiah! In verse 41 see Jesus weeping over the city that He loves! Are we going to allow the stones to cry out because we as God's people are too shy and timid to praise our God? I've made a choice to praise Him continually and I know that as I do so, I do my little part of filling the earth "with the glory of the Lord" (Numbers 14:21).

The psalmist says in Psalm 69:30-31:

"I will praise the name of God with a song;
I will magnify Him with thanksgiving. This
will please the Lord more than an ox or a
bull with horns and hoofs."

When my 82-year-old mom slipped into a coma, she was transferred to the intensive care unit of the hospital. I knew it was her time to go and be with Jesus. We sang our songs of praise and thanksgiving around her, lifting up the name of Jesus. The nurses came and told us that those were the most beautiful songs they had ever heard, and to please continue. The family next to us later told us that they were Christians, and that our praises had really ministered to them as they said their last good-byes to their loved one. We had such a joy as we walked through the difficult time of seeing our mom depart from planet earth! But the joy of the Lord is our strength! (Nehemiah 8:10) It's His joy inside of us, not coming from the world or from any other source, but from the Holy Spirit inside of us. Mom's funeral Mass was a celebration; it was a time of praise to the Lord for her life and for the fact that she had made it to the finish line. (2 Timothy 4:7) Now she was in glory! As my sister and I praised the Lord, we were filled with joy and gladness. A young man who attended the funeral Mass went back home and told his mom that he now believed for certain the promises of Jesus, because he knew how close we were to mom and in spite of her death we could still rejoice and be glad. Thank you, Jesus! There were Christians of other denominations in mom's Mass, who were so touched by the Holy Spirit, that they told my sister that they had never attended such a Spirit-filled service as this one! But doesn't the Word of God say that he inhabits our praises? (Ps.22:3) And when He does there is a change in the atmosphere. It's our choice to remain in self-pity and sadness or to enter into His presence, where there is fullness of joy! (Ps. 16:11) As the psalmist says in Psalm 113:3 "From the rising of the sun to its setting the name of the Lord is to be praised!" Amen!

Praise is a powerful weapon against our enemies. The Scriptures talk about putting on the garment of praise (Isaiah 61:3); this garment of praise happens to be a "demon-repellent!" Where there is powerful praise in our mouths, what Psalm 149:6 calls "the high praises of God," the Lord moves in power against our enemies. Our praises become "two-edged swords" in God's hands and the enemy is defeated. Read 2 Chronicles 20:1-30; it's a powerful story of how the Lord uses our praises against our enemies. No matter how strong the enemy is "the battle is not yours but God's" (v.15), and He takes our praises and uses them to defeat the enemy. In one of my trips to Ghana I was faced with a demonic attack of discouragement as I entered my room. All I can say is, that suddenly, I didn't want to be in Ghana, I didn't want to preach and I wanted to go back home. I knew that this was not me, but something coming against me; therefore I put into action what I knew: I put on my garment of praise and started to praise the Lord and dance in that room; I praised Him in English, in Spanish and in tongues; I took authority against the enemy and continued praising until there was a breakthrough and I experienced a release from that attack. I went to bed free and in peace. Thank you, Jesus! The next day I preached at a conference and many people came to Jesus and got filled with the Holy Spirit. Peter says in 1Peter 5:9

"Resist him, firm in your faith...."

Praise is one of the best ways that we stay on track as we wait on God, because it helps us to keep our focus on the Lord. In His presence we are changed:

> "And we all, with unveiled face, beholding the glory of the
> Lord, are being changed into His likeness from one degree
> of glory to another; for this comes from the Lord who is
> the Spirit." (2Corinthians 3:18)

4. Remember!

"I will call to mind the deeds of the Lord; yea, I will remember thy wonders of old. I will meditate on all thy work, and muse on

75

thy mighty deeds." (Ps. 77:11-12)

Stop the worrying and remind yourself of how the Lord has delivered you in the past; the same God who delivered you ten years ago, five years ago, one year ago, will deliver you again. The same God that delivered you in 1987 will deliver you in 2004 and 2010. He's still seated on the throne and has not lost an ounce of power. He's not biting His nails! He's not worried! I just love what Corrie Ten Boom says: "There are no problems in heaven, just plans!" Learn to take "every thought captive to obey Christ" (2 Cor. 10:5). The enemy is an expert in lying to us; our minds are the battleground! The enemy is not omniscient, but he can certainly send lies and negativity into our minds. Jesus called him in John 8:44 "a liar and a father of lies." The enemy's nature is to lie and sow deception and fear into our minds. He speaks lies to us and we believe them, thinking that those thoughts originated with us. Many times we take action based on those lies instead of discerning and taking every thought "captive" to obey Christ. It boils down to this: whose report are you going to believe? As God's people, we must choose to believe the Word of God and stand on that Word! In the midst of his trouble, the psalmist says in Ps. 77:5:

"I consider the days of old,
I remember the years long ago."

Knowing how the Lord dealt with His people and delivered them again and again helps us to remember His faithfulness to us; He is a covenant-keeping God. At one point in my life I didn't know where I would live with my four children. We had to move out of our rented house and I had no idea where we would go. My estranged husband was not very communicative and we had just experienced a financial disaster. I could trust only the Lord for a place to live. I remembered how He had come through with a buyer for our previous house in the midst of a real estate crisis. I reminded Him of His word in Matthew 6:33:

"But seek first his kingdom and his righteousness,

and all these things shall be yours as well."

My knees shook with fear, my teeth ached and my eyes twitched, but I kept remembering that He is a faithful God who "hears the needy and does not despise his own that are in bonds." Ps. 69:33 The Lord came through again and brought us into a beautiful home on a lake. Truly, He is "able to do far more abundantly than all that we ask or think…!" (Ephesians 3:20) Amen!

The psalmist in Ps.78: 4-7 exhorts us to:

"tell to the coming generation the glorious deeds of the Lord, and his might, and the wonders which he has wrought…so that they should set their hope on God, and not forget the works of God, but keep His commandments…."

This is why the Lord was so insistent that His people, the Israelites, would celebrate feasts remembering His great and mighty deeds so that the coming generations would not forget Him. Calling to mind the greatness of our God and remembering His personal words to us will help us to stay on track as we wait on Him. The psalmist says in Ps. 111:2 "Great are the works of the Lord, studied by all who have pleasure in them." Spending time studying the works of Jesus will profit us (and our families) far more than what we can imagine. "Jesus Christ is the same yesterday and today and for ever" (Hebrews 13:8); we can count on the fact that He still saves, delivers and heals! Remember what His Word says! His Word is more real than what we see with our eyes! The Apostle Paul says in 2 Cor. 4:17-18:

"For this slight momentary affliction is preparing for us an
eternal weight of glory beyond all comparison, because
we look not to the things that are seen but to the things
that are unseen; for the things that are unseen are eternal."

Remember that what we don't see with our natural eyes is what's really real. My friend Annie, pregnant with her fifth child, was told by the doctors that her baby was not growing well; that it was tiny and not normal. The doctors told her the baby would die. We laid hands on her proclaiming the healing power of Jesus and reminded the Lord of His covenant of healing for His people. We broke the power of the negative words spoken over the baby's life and we spoke life and healing into the baby's life. In moments of discouragement and of "negative reports," Annie would remind herself of what the Scriptures reveal about healing:

"That He took our infirmities and bore our diseases" (Matthew 8:17) and

"By His wounds you have been healed." (1 Peter 2:24)

The baby was born prematurely, but today she is a healthy two-year-old! Thank you, Jesus!

Remember to remind God of His promises. Isaiah 62:6-7 says:

"Upon your walls, O Jerusalem, I have set watchmen;
all the day and all the night they shall never be silent.
You who put the Lord in remembrance, take no rest,
and give him no rest until He establishes Jerusalem
and makes it a praise in the earth."

The Lord says to put Him in remembrance, to give Him no rest! Does this mean He has a bad memory and that He forgets? NO! He wants to see His people calling out to Him in complete dependence on Him and Him alone. "His delight is not in the strength of the horse, nor his pleasure in the legs of a man; but the Lord takes pleasure in those who fear Him, in those who hope in his steadfast love." (Ps. 147:10-11)

There is an inheritance that the Lord Jesus won for us at Calvary that we should always keep in mind; in this way we will not act like "orphans," as if we didn't have a Father who has already provided for all our needs. Ps. 103:2-6 tells us to:

"Forget not all His benefits, who forgives all your iniquity, who heals all your diseases, who redeems your life from the pit, who crowns you with steadfast love and mercy, who satisfies you with good as long as you live so that your youth is renewed like the eagle's. The Lord works vindication and justice for all who are oppressed."

These are some of His most important benefits, and we are supposed to remember them! However, it is difficult to remember God's promises if we are entertained constantly by the soaps and other T.V. programs! We need to make a daily choice as to how we're going to spend our time. We don't want to be like Esau, who traded his inheritance for a plate of lentils! (Genesis 25:29-34)

# ADD FASTING TO YOUR PRAYERS!

"And when you fast...." (Matthew 6:16)

The Lord Jesus assumes that as His followers we would not only pray, but also fast. To fast is to voluntarily abstain from food, in order to focus on Him as our source. It's a way of humbling ourselves before the Lord. A biblical principle to keep in mind is that "God opposes the proud but gives grace to the humble." (1 Peter 5:5b) Humility is the door through which grace flows into our lives. Fasting is a way of telling the Lord "I'm really serious about this situation; I'm desperate and You're the only one that can help!" Throughout the Scriptures we see God's people humbling themselves before Him in prayer and fasting. Even though there are different reasons for fasting, one thing remains the same: only He can help. When King Jehoshaphat was facing three enemy armies more powerful than his, he turned to the Lord in prayer and fasting (2 Chronicles 20:3). He realized that he was powerless in this battle and turned to the Lord for help:

> "...for we are powerless against this great multitude
> That is coming against us. We do not know what
> To do, but our eyes are upon thee."

The Lord gave His people a mighty victory over the enemy, by releasing the strategy on how to win the battle and releasing confusion on the enemy.

Do you ever feel powerless when you are facing situations that are just beyond your control? Have you reached that point in your life that you know that only the Lord can turn the situation around? You're in a good place for a miracle! Try prayer and fasting!

Another beautiful and powerful example of fasting is found in Ezra 8. As exiled Jews were returning to Jerusalem, Ezra called for a fast.

> "Then I proclaimed a fast there, at the river Ahava, that
> we might humble ourselves before our God, to seek from

Him a straight way for ourselves, our children, and all our goods." (Ezra 8:21)

This fast was for guidance and protection on their journey, including their children and possessions. Ezra led his people to fast because of "the enemy on our way." (v.21) At the conclusion of the journey he was able to say that "…the hand of our God was upon us, and He delivered us from the hand of the enemy and from ambushes by the way." Once again we see that through prayer and fasting the Lord releases victory over the enemy. As we press on into God's plan for our lives, we will encounter enemies on the road (a negative report, fear, anxiety, confusion, lies and deception, etc.) that will harass us and try to hinder us from entering into our destiny. At times the enemy releases all kind of difficulties so that we won't even make it to prayer group! Flat tires, car accidents, headaches, phone calls, broken appliances are some of his ambushes so that we "skip" prayer group just that "one time." It never ceases to amaze me how so often when we're leading someone to the Lord, suddenly, all kinds of distractions are released against us; the phone rings, the dog needs to go outside, the children start arguing and the baby falls. All at the same time! As we continue to rely on Him and make praying with fasting a discipline in our lives, the Lord will give us the victory over every plan and strategy of the enemy to keep us off track.

Jesus, our model, after His baptism in the Holy Spirit fasted in the desert for forty days where He was tempted by the devil (Luke 4:1-2). Luke writes that "Jesus, full of the Holy Spirit, returned from the Jordan, and was led by the Spirit for forty days in the wilderness, tempted by the devil. And He ate nothing in those days…." It's interesting that Luke mentions that after He left the wilderness, where Jesus defeated the enemy:

"… Jesus returned in the power of the Spirit…."

There's a difference between being "full of the Spirit" and being "in the power of the Spirit." Something happened to Jesus as He prayed and fasted in the wilderness: there was a release of power.

Fasting helps us to overcome the enemy by releasing faith and Holy Spirit power in our lives. Jesus' ministry certainly manifested the power of the Holy Spirit through the accompanying signs of miracles, wonders, healing, and deliverances. In Mark 9, when the disciples could not cast out an evil spirit out of a boy, they asked Jesus why they were unable. Jesus told them in v.29:

> "This kind cannot be driven out by anything but prayer and fasting."

When God's people faced extermination (Esther 3:8-9; 13), Queen Esther decided she had to intervene and approach the king even at the cost of her life. However, before doing so she called for a fast.

> "Go, gather all the Jews to be found in Susa, and hold a fast on my behalf, and neither eat nor drink for three days, night or day. I and my maids will also fast as you do. Then I will go to the king, though it is against the law; and if I perish, I perish." (Esther 4:16)

The corporate fasting by the Jews turned the situation completely around; the Jews were preserved and the enemy was hanged instead (Esther 7:10). The victory was so profound that not only was the enemy defeated, but a complete reversal took place: Mordecai the Jew was promoted to next in rank to the king! (Esther 10:3)

So far we have seen that fasting moves the powerful hand of God, releasing deliverance and victory for God's people. It also releases faith and Holy Spirit power in our individual lives to resist and defeat the enemy. God intervenes on our behalf for our good and His glory. However, there is even more that the Lord releases into our lives as we humble ourselves with prayer and fasting. The story of Jonah with the Ninevites (Israel's wicked enemies) deserves to be mentioned because the Lord's great mercy was released instead of judgment when they repented and humbled themselves before God with fasting. Because of Jonah's preaching

"...the people of Nineveh believed God; they proclaimed a fast, and put on sackcloth, from the greatest of them to the least of them." Even the king fasted and said "...yea, let every one turn from his evil way and from the violence which is in his hands. Who knows, God may yet repent and turn from his fierce anger, so that we perish not?" (Jonah 3:8-9) I believe that demonic strongholds were dealt with as the people humbled themselves before God. They realized that they had to change their ways and turn to God. It's called repentance. Isn't it time that we humble ourselves corporately, with prayer and fasting, for the Church in America? Isn't it time to repent for pride and arrogance, abortion, violence and sexual abuse, complacency and lukewarmness, greed and materialism, addictions of every kind? Isn't it time to repent for the way that the Gospel has been diluted? Let's learn from the Ninevites and:

"Seek the Lord while He may be found, call upon Him while He is near; let the wicked forsake his way, and the unrighteous man his thoughts; let him return to the Lord, that He may have mercy on him, and to our God, for He will abundantly pardon." (Isaiah 55:6-7)

Fasting somehow brings clarity and truth into our lives so that we desire to reject evil and seek the wholeness that only comes through God. It helps us to pull down the strongholds in our minds and to "take every thought captive to obey Christ...." (2 Corinthians 10:5)

The early Church prayed and fasted when seeking direction from the Lord and they received it. In Acts 13:2-3 it says:

"While they were worshipping the Lord and fasting, the Holy Spirit said, Set apart for me Barnabas and Saul for the work to which I have called them. Then after fasting and praying they laid their hands on them and sent them off."

It was the Holy Spirit Himself that set apart Barnabas and Saul and anointed them for the work God had chosen them for. It was not a man-made decision, but God's. God called them and sent them off equipped with Holy Spirit power to carry on God's work with the same anointing Jesus manifested during His ministry: signs, wonders, healings, miracles. They preached, healed the sick, cast out demons, resurrected the dead. Fasting helps to birth the signs that follow the preaching of the gospel (Mark 16:17-18). As a result of fasting, the Lord gave a clear word to set apart Barnabas and Saul; after fasting they prayed and laid hands on them for their work and the two missionaries left with the Holy Spirit empowerment for their work.

It's important to keep a clean heart and right relationships when fasting. Isaiah 58 gives a description of the kind of fast that pleases God. There is revelation, healing, protection, answered prayer, promise of His presence, joy, guidance, satisfaction, strength, refreshment, restoration, and exaltation when we fast the way that pleases Him.

Once I understood the necessity of fasting in my life, I have disciplined myself, with the help of the Holy Spirit, to completely fast from food once a week. I also do extended fasts as the Holy Spirits directs. I have seen great victories and answered prayers from the weekly fasts that I do with my friend Cristina. Let me share some of them:

• My son Eddy was surprised by how many medical schools accepted him!
• Cristina's son, who had been diagnosed with severe learning disabilities, is now finishing his Masters degree at American University, without medicines.
• My son Ricky got the job he desired, in God's perfect timing.
• Protection of my "possessions" as they lay in storage for almost
 three years.
• Victory in court as the judge set aside a mediated, signed, divorce settlement agreement. (This was a first in a Dade County Court!)
• Breakthrough in mediation proceedings. I walked out of mediation with a lump sum instead of monthly alimony payments. This has caused great peace, joy and freedom for me.
• Normal growth and development for a baby that had been diag-

nosed with Down's Syndrome.
- Protection for our children away in college.
- Protection in my journeys.
- Many people repenting and committing their lives to Jesus.

Personally, through fasting I have experienced a greater desire to do His will, a greater desire for His presence, a greater desire to hear His voice. I have seen a release of faith in moments of great need. I have seen the enemies of fear, anxiety and discouragement defeated again and again. Demonic strongholds of anger and resentment have been shattered and I'm experiencing a greater freedom in the Spirit .

Dear reader, I pray that the Holy Spirit has already convinced you of your need to pray with fasting, for the kingdom is taken over "by force" (Matthew 11:12).

# STAY ROOTED IN THE
# HOUSE OF THE LORD

"The righteous flourish like the palm tree, and grow like a cedar in Lebanon. They are planted in the house of the Lord, they flourish in the courts of our God. They still bring forth fruit in old age, they are ever full of sap and green...." Ps. 92:12-14

Do you want to bear fruit even into "old age"? You must belong to a Church and form part of a community of believers. We are not to be isolated; we are meant to flourish and grow within a group. According to the above passage, it's in the context of a congregation that we flourish, grow and become fruitful, even in our old age! As Catholics we have the privilege of daily Mass if we so choose. The Apostle John says in 1 John 1:7:

"but if we walk in the light, as he is in the light,
we have fellowship with one another...."

If we are walking with Jesus, we will have fellowship with those who are walking with Him, too. We are part of His body. 1 John 5:1(b) says "and every one who loves the parent loves the child." If we love our heavenly Father we love His children!

The writer of Hebrews says:

"and let us consider how to stir up one another to love and good works, not neglecting to meet together, as is the habit of some, but encouraging one another, and all the more as you see the Day drawing near." (Hebrews 10:25)

One of the devil's best tactics is to have believers isolate themselves from a community because of being hurt or ignored. Once a person quits being a member of a community, usually there will not be much growth in the Spirit, because the ways of the Spirit are more "caught than taught." Only with others can "iron sharpen iron" (Proverbs 27:17) as we learn to love and accept those people who "get on our nerves." The Lord has given us the gifts of the Holy Spirit so that we can build and extend His kingdom. The gift of prophecy is tailor-made to upbuild, encourage and console (1Cor.14:3). The Lord knew that we would need encouragement and consolation when facing battles, difficulties and delays! In 2 Chronicles 20, King Jehoshaphat is facing an impossible situation: he's being attacked by three enemy armies more powerful than he. Verse 4 says that "Judah assembled to seek help from the Lord; from all the cities of Judah they came to seek the Lord." In other words, the people got together to seek the face of the Lord; they didn't stay isolated in their homes. It was in that setting that the Spirit of the Lord came upon a prophet and he was able to give a "Word" from God to the king and the people. This "Word" encouraged, comforted and directed them. In verse 15 the Lord said:

"Thus says the Lord to you, fear not, and be not dismayed
at this great multitude; for the battle is not yours but God's."

What a "Word!" Then the prophet gave instructions to meet the enemy. There was victory over the enemy in Judah's camp, as they heeded the prophetic word. King Jehoshaphat told his army in verse 20

"Believe in the Lord your God and you will be established;
believe his prophets, and you will succeed."

There is a "corporate" anointing that you won't receive if you stay at home.

The good news is that as believers, we "can all prophesy"(1 Corinthians 14:31). In other words, by the Spirit we are all able to hear God and speak it forth. John 10:3 says that "the sheep hear his voice." If Jesus is your shepherd, you can hear His voice! On the day of Pentecost, when the Holy Spirit was poured, Peter quoted from the prophet Joel, saying:

"And in the last days it shall be, God declares,
that I will pour out my Spirit
upon all flesh, and your sons and your daughters shall
PROPHESY…." (Acts 2:17)

Do you have the Holy Spirit? Then, according to God's Word, you can prophesy! You can have a "word" that will strengthen, comfort, and console His Body. (1 Corinthians 14:3) It's powerful when you go to prayer group and the prophetic Word seems to be specifically designed for you. And it is! The Lord knows you intimately and knows what you need to hear! Years ago, just before I was getting a colonoscopy, I attended the healing service at the charismatic conference in Miami. The priest got a word of knowledge saying that there were some people in the audience who would be going through medical procedures in their intestines, but the Lord wanted them to know that they were okay. That was me! What a relief to know that my intestines were okay! I received that "Word" as truly from God's throne. I went through the procedure with peace and comfort knowing that I was okay. And I was!

My brother Rene did not know Jesus personally, but he was "searching." It was at a Charismatic Mass given in thanksgiving for my first book "There's Power in Your Tongue," that he was sovereignly baptized in the Holy Spirit and received the gift of tongues. He says that as he heard us sing in tongues, the language of the Holy Spirit, he thought to himself that those were the most beautiful sounds he had ever heard. He said to the Lord that he wanted it, and the Holy Spirit responded just as in Pentecost! (Acts 2) His life has changed since that moment. He has committed his life to the Lord Jesus Christ and is now filled with the joy of the Lord and witnessing to all! The point is that when God's people get together in His name, expect something to happen, because Jesus has promised that He will be in our midst. (Matthew 18:20) No wonder the enemy keeps so many people away from the community of believers!

According to Ps. 133, it's when "brothers dwell in unity" that "there the Lord has commanded the blessing, life for evermore." In the place of unity with other believers, the Lord moves with power and glory. Not only are there physical, mental and emotional healings that take place as we praise and worship Him, but I can testify that my blurry vision has been adjusted time and time again in the midst of a delay as I waited for the promise. I have been encouraged and comforted. The prophetic words and songs, the words of knowledge and wisdom, the Scripture readings and teachings in the group have helped me stay on track. Getting together with our brothers and sisters in the faith is a must to make it into our "destiny." If you don't belong to a prayer group, I encourage you to find one where the "high praises of God" exist! It's there that the Lord takes those high praises and changes them into "two-edged swords" against the enemy! (Ps. 149:6)

> "...let us run with perseverance the race that is set before us, looking to Jesus, the pioneer and perfecter of our faith...."
> (Hebrews 12:1b-2)

# DON'T COME BEFORE
# HIM EMPTY-HANDED!

"They shall not appear before the Lord empty-handed;
every man shall give as he is able, according to the blessing of the Lord your God which he has given you." (Deut.
16:16-17)

It's important that guided by the Holy Spirit we give to the work
of the Lord. It's not that we can manipulate God with our giving;
we cannot (Acts 8:20). But as God's people our finances must be
under the Lordship of Jesus Christ. John 3:16 says that:

" For God so loved the world that He gave...."

God gave and sent His most precious gift to us so that we could
be saved. Now we give back to Him out of love! The Holy Spirit
creates in us generous hearts so that we can give to the Lord's work
and to those in need, as the Holy Spirit leads. We're used to tipping
the Lord! But tithing started with Father Abraham (Genesis 14:20).
Tithings and offerings are laws set by God, not man. When we give
to the Lord, we are sowing into His kingdom and at the right time
we shall reap. The apostle Paul says in 2 Corinthians 9:6 :

"The point is this: he who sows sparingly
will also reap sparingly, and he who
sows bountifully will also reap bountifully."

Giving my tithes and offerings has caused great joy in my heart
because I know I'm pleasing Him and through them I'm blessing
the Church and God's people as I do so. Recently in prayer group
the Holy Spirit pointed out a lady to me who needed financial help;
I just knew that she had a need. At the time of intercession I prayed
that the Lord would meet everyone's financial need who was present in that room. To my surprise I heard the voice of the Lord tell
me, "You help her." I wrote out a check and gave it to her; she had
tears in her eyes. When she got home she found a notice in her

door that her water supply would be shut off that day if she didn't pay. The money for the water bill came just in time and the Lord used me to bless her. I just thanked the Lord that I heard His voice and I obeyed! Many times we pray for hurricane and earthquake victims in other countries, while next to us there are people in great need going through their own personal hurricanes and earthquakes and because our ears are not open to the Lord's voice, we miss it! We miss the chance to be used by the Lord to bless the people that He loves!

Tithing has given me a greater sense of security in the Lord because of the great promises attached to it in Malachi 3:10-12. It's amazing that in this passage of Scripture the Lord says to test Him when it comes to tithing:

> "Bring the full tithes into the storehouse, that there may be food in my house; and thereby put Me to the test, says the Lord of Hosts, if I will not open the windows of heaven for you and pour down for you an overflowing blessing. I will rebuke the devourer for you, so that it will not destroy the fruits of your soil; and your vine in the field shall not fail to bear, says the Lord of Hosts. Then all nations will call you blessed, for you will be a land of delight, says the Lord of hosts."

Let's take a brief look at these awesome promises:

1. When we tithe, there will be "food in My house" to feed His people. Jesus quoted from Deuteronomy 8:3 when tempted by the devil and said "Man shall not live by bread alone, but by every word that proceeds from the mouth of God." We need the truth, light, strength, comfort, guidance, conviction and wisdom that comes only from the Word of God. As God's people, we're supposed to walk by faith; faith comes by hearing the preaching of the Word (Romans 10:17). In the Catholic Church we're blessed to have the real presence of Jesus in the Eucharist; this does not negate the fact that we also are supposed to "eat" the Word of God! It's not one or the other, it's both! The choice is

ours: poor tithing, poor food; good tithing, great food. Imagine the day that we wake up corporately and start giving our tithes; the Church will explode with great faith and power!

2. When we tithe, the Lord will "open the windows of heaven" for us. This means that the Holy Spirit will give us new revelation, ideas, concepts, methods to prosper us so that we can make it into our destiny. I totally attribute to tithing the fact that I'm writing books! I'm not a writer; this is something I never enjoyed. However, the Holy Spirit is the one giving me revelation to write books that will edify His people. Whatever your profession, the "windows of heaven" will be opened for you as you tithe.

3. When we tithe, the Lord will "pour down for you an overflowing blessing." Our needs will be met; there will be no more need. When we give we place ourselves in a position to receive His blessings. He will not only bless us; He will do so abundantly!

4. When we tithe, He "will rebuke the devourer for you, so that it will not destroy the fruits of your soil." The Lord Himself will deal with the devil and kick him out of our lives when he comes to attack. There is protection for our lives, our finances, our businesses from the attacks of the enemy. I could write a book just on this!

5. When we tithe, "your vine in the field shall not fail to bear." Our children will be fruitful and they will prosper in life: spiritually, financially, emotionally, etc. This verse is a great one to stand on when we intercede for our children and grandchildren!

6. When we tithe, "all nations will call you blessed." The Hebrew word used here for blessed is the word "ashar." It means happy, blessed, prosperous, successful, straight, right, contented.

7. When we tithe, "you will be a land of delight." The favor of

God will be on us and everyone will see and know that our God is with us. People will be drawn to us because "the glory of the Lord is risen upon you." (Isaiah 60:1)

Let me share a story with you. For years my mother, my sister, our friends prayed for my brother's conversion. About a year and a half before mom passed away I encouraged her to plant financial seeds in ministries where the Gospel was preached in the power of the Spirit; where people were repenting and committing their lives to Jesus. She faithfully planted in various ministries as she interceded for my brother's salvation. Exactly five months after mom passed away, my brother committed his life to Jesus! I believe that mom's faith in the Lord for my brother's salvation was released through her financial giving and the enemy was rebuked from my brother's life. Thank you, Jesus!

It's interesting to note that when the centurion in Luke 7 needed a healing for his servant, the Jews tell Jesus in v.5 that:

"He is worthy to have you do this for him, for he loves our nation, and he built us our synagogue."

The Roman centurion, out of love (he had the right motive), built a synagogue for the Jews. Now, to build a synagogue takes money. How did Jesus answer? Verse 6 says that "Jesus went with them." The rest of the story is that Jesus just "says the Word" and the servant is healed.

In Acts 10, the Gospel is taken to the Gentiles by Peter, a Jew. Now, a good Jew would never go inside the home of a Gentile! But Peter was ordered by the Holy Spirit to do so. The Gospel was also for the Gentiles! Jesus died for them as well and Peter is God's messenger to proclaim the good news to them! Who is this Gentile man Cornelius? He is a Roman centurion, "a devout man who feared God with all his household, gave alms liberally to the people, and prayed constantly to God." (v.2) Cornelius had been giving money to the poor and it caught God's attention. In a vision Cornelius sees an angel who tells him (v.4) "Your prayers and your alms have ascended as a memorial before God." In verse 31, as Cornelius is recounting his story, it says "Cornelius, your prayer has been heard and your alms have been remembered before God." Three times in the same chapter the Holy Spirit underlines the fact that Cornelius was a giver! (v.2,4,31)

Paul says that "God loves a cheerful giver" (2 Corinthians 9:7b). When we give out of a grateful and generous heart to God, He takes notice. Jesus certainly noticed the poor widow in Mark 12:41-44 as she put into the treasury two copper coins; she gave out of her poverty. She had nothing left! Another woman who captured the heart of God was Mary of Bethany (Matthew 26:6-13). She poured on Jesus a "very expensive ointment," which brought criticism from the disciples. They thought it was a waste and they were indignant. They could not understand why she had "wasted" such expensive perfume on Him; they had their own ideas of how to use the money! However, Jesus was so pleased with Mary's extravagant giving, that He said "Truly, I say to you, wherever this gospel is preached in the whole world, what she has done will be told in memory of her."

Psalm 20 is a prayer that was proclaimed before going to war. In verses 3-4 the people say:

"May He remember all your offerings and regard
with favor your burnt offerings. May He grant
you your heart's desire, and fulfill all your plans!"

Again we see the relationship between giving and receiving God's help. Are there any battles you are facing?

In 2 Samuel 24, King David disobeyed the Lord by taking a census and the Lord sent a plague that killed 70,000 men. David was distraught when he saw the angel stretch forth his hand toward Jerusalem to destroy it. He cried out to the Lord. The prophet Gad came to David with God's Word and instructed him to "Go up, rear an altar to the Lord on the threshing floor of Araunah the Jebusite." What do you do in an altar? It's a place of sacrifice! You sacrifice something of value; if not, it's not a sacrifice. In verses 21-22 Araunah said "Why has my lord my king come to his servant?"

David said, "To buy the threshing floor of you, in order to build an altar to the Lord, that the plague may be averted from the people." Araunah wanted to give everything to the king for free; the oxen for the sacrifice, the threshing sledges and the yokes of the oxen for the wood. Let's look at David's response in v.24.

"But the king said to Araunah, No,
but I will buy it of you for a price;
I will not offer burnt offerings to the
Lord my God which cost me nothing."

It's really when our giving costs us something that the Lord is touched by it. After David built the altar and offered the offerings, the Lord heeded his supplications and "the plague was averted from Israel." (v.25.) Something is set in motion in the Spirit as we give to the Lord something that "costs" us and is dear to us.

Will you allow the Holy Spirit to search you and show you where to give and how much? *Yes,*

# PASS THE TEST OF UNFORGIVENESS

"Lord, when my brother wrongs me, how often must I forgive him? Seven times? No, Jesus replied, not seven times; I say, seventy times seven times." ( Matthew 18:21-22)

As you see from Jesus' words, forgiveness is continuous in our lives. It's not a suggestion, but a command. Jesus Himself forgave us from the Cross as He said (Luke 23:34):

"Father, forgive them; for they know not what they do."

It's crucial that we forgive in order to move forward with the Lord. Unforgiveness may keep us "stuck," preventing us from entering into our destiny. In one of my preaching trips I was asked by a friend to go and pray with a sick lady, who at one point in her life had served the Lord with great zeal. I prayed in the Spirit before my visit and the Lord showed me a root of bitterness in this lady. As it turned out, this lady had serious health problems; she had gone through many surgeries in her stomach with another surgery coming up. Years before she had led youth groups with great power and anointing and was responsible for many people coming to the Lord. She had been used mightily by God. However, she had gotten very angry with a good friend, who happened to be a priest. She nursed her anger and became bitter. She eventually became sicker and sicker and quit serving God. As I prayed and ministered to her, she forgave her friend and I felt that she should call him up and make peace with him. Then I asked her, "Sister, does this word from Jeremiah 1:5 ring a bell?

"Before I formed you in the womb I knew you,
and before you were born I consecrated you;
I appointed you a prophet to the nations"

Her eyes lit up and said "That's the word spoken over my life when I came to Jesus!" I told her: "Sister, the same calling is still on you; pick up where you left off and move into your destiny."

Here was a prophetess of God "stuck" for years because of unforgiveness, but as soon as she forgave she was "unstuck!" She called the priest and they have reconciled. Thank you, Jesus!

Jesus says in Mark 11:25:

"And whenever you stand praying, forgive,
if you have anything against any one;
so that your Father also who is in heaven
may forgive you your trespasses."

Unforgiveness hinders our prayer lives and is an open door to demonic attacks as well. In Matthew 18:34 (NKJ) the servant who refused to show mercy to his fellow servant by forgiving his debt was handed over to the "torturers" by his master. What do you think "torturers" do? They torture people! Depression and despair, fear and panic attacks, anxiety, sickness and disease, confusion and insanity are all part of the "torture package." As we wait on the Lord it's important that we forgive and let go of anger and resentment; we must "shut the door" on the enemy's face because the last thing we want is more torment and attacks on our lives. Our lives must be aligned to the Word of God, and when unforgiveness is revealed let's deal with it right away. This "test" of forgiveness we must pass because all of us have been hurt by others. It's not natural for us to forgive, but with the grace of God we are able to do so! God's grace is sufficient!

Joseph, Jacob's son, was betrayed and sold into slavery by his own brothers. (Genesis 37:27) God had given him dreams of a great destiny but before he entered into God's promise he was taken to Egypt as a slave and eventually landed in prison for a crime he did not commit. His brothers sold him when he was a teen, and it was at age 30 (Genesis 41: 46) that he became the prime minister of Egypt. He spent many years "waiting" for God's vision for his life come to pass, but there was one important test that he needed to pass: forgiveness. It's interesting to note the name he gave his first born son: Manasseh, which means "making forgetful."

"For God has made me forget all my hardship and all my
father's house." (Genesis 41:51)

Joseph, a type of Jesus, forgave his brothers and was able to tell
them in Genesis 50:20 "But as for you, you meant evil against me;
but God meant it for good...." The name of his second son was
Ephraim, meaning

"For God has made me fruitful in the land of my affliction."
(Genesis 41:52)

In order to be "fruitful" we must first forgive! Forgiveness comes
before fruitfulness!

David had to pass the same test of forgiving his enemy, King
Saul. David had the opportunity of killing him several times, but he
didn't, even though his own men were trying to persuade him to do
so. David told his men "The Lord forbid that I should do this thing
to my lord, the Lord's anointed, to put forth my hand against him,
seeing he is the Lord's anointed. So David persuaded his men with
these words, and did not permit them to attack Saul." (1 Samuel
24:6-7) It's obvious from these two stories that we must forgive!
It's part of God's vision for us to be a forgiving people! In order to
move to our next level we must pass the "test" of forgiveness. In a
sense, we must give thanks to the Lord for our enemies, for because
of them we enter into our destiny as we move in forgiveness!

"But I say to you that hear, love your enemies, do good
to those who hate you, bless those who curse you, pray
for those who abuse you." (Luke 6:27-28)

Will you do that now?

# PROPHESY AND PROCLAIM, DECREE AND DECLARE

"You will also declare a thing and it will be established for you...." (Job 22:28) (NKJ)

Is the vision or promise burning in your heart? Then you know where the Lord wants to take you. It's crucial that at this moment you realize the importance of the right (and wrong) use of your tongue. We have tremendous power in the tongue! (Proverbs 18:21) Your tongue acts in the same way as a bit in the horse's mouth and as a rudder in a ship; it basically controls where you want to go. Amazing! James says in 3:3-4:

"If we put bits into the mouths of horses that they may obey us, we guide their whole bodies. Look at the ships also; though they are so great and are driven by strong winds, they are guided by a very small rudder wherever the will of the pilot directs."

In the same way, the tongue is a small member of the body but has tremendous power to get us or not to get us into our "destiny." Even in the midst of "strong winds" the tongue is a mighty weapon to take us where we're supposed to land. So use your tongue as a bit or rudder to get you into your "destiny." Now, James says that "no human being can tame the tongue—a restless evil, full of deadly poison." (James 3:8) We have no other choice than to surrender our tongue to the Holy Spirit and ask Him to help us use our tongues correctly. Speak words that bring life into your dream or vision. Remember, the Lord has a specific plan for your life here on earth. It's in this plan that the Lord will be greatly glorified in you and through you; this is where you experience His joy and the power and fruit of the Holy Spirit as you fulfill His plan for your life. This is the place of fruitfulness.

Agree with the Lord, according to His Word; stand on the Word and do not waver. Remember, we walk by faith and not by sight; do not allow the waves of difficulties and the winds of adversity to change your mind:

> "...for you know that the testing of your faith produces steadfastness. And let steadfastness have its full effect, that you may be perfect and complete, lacking in nothing" (James 1:3-4).

Our faith must mature. The temptation when things don't go our way, what is common to our flesh, is to grumble, complain, accuse, point the finger or to become negative. Don't fall into this deadly trap! Using the tongue in this way will attract the serpents and scorpions (despair, discouragement, fear, anxiety) and it will be much harder to keep your eyes fixed on the Lord. Instead use your tongue to decree, declare and proclaim the great plans, the victory, the breakthrough that the Lord has in store for you. Prophesy over your vision! The muscles of faith must be developed and stretched! If you have the Holy Spirit, you can prophesy! (1 Cor. 14:31; Acts 2:17-18) We need the prophetic word! It confirms and guides us in difficult moments. "Without prophecy the people become demoralized...." (Proverbs 29:18 NAB) Without vision it's easy to become complacent, get off track and become neutralized. Believing the prophetic word enables one to engage in spiritual warfare with confidence, knowing that what the Lord has spoken will be fulfilled. The Apostle Paul writes to Timothy:

> "This charge I commit to you, Timothy, my son,
>          in accordance with the prophetic utterances
> which pointed to you, that inspired by them you may wage
> the good warfare...." (1 Timothy 1:18)

Decree and declare that prophetic word over your destiny! You have "rivers of living water" flowing inside of you (John 7:38) and "the voice of the Lord is upon the waters...." (Ps. 29:3) Listen to His voice!

The time of waiting or delay is not the time to waver in unbelief; allow the Lord to strengthen your heart as you press on. Ps. 27:13-14 says:

"I believe that I will see the goodness of the Lord in the land of the living! Wait for the Lord; be strong, and let your heart take courage; yea, wait for the Lord!"

Remember Abraham, who used his tongue to give glory to God, and as he did, "he grew strong in his faith" as he waited for Isaac (Romans 4:20).

It was in 1996 that the Lord gave me a vision of "The Glory of God." In this vision I saw a one-story house with a flat roof; the Lord showed me exactly where I should place a Cross and told me to name this place "The Glory of God." I believe this is a place where the glory of God will be revealed; that it will be a place of grace, where people can be delivered, set free, healed, saved, restored. It will be a place where they can find Jesus. It will be a place where the power of the Gospel can be demonstrated (1 Corinthians 4:20). I started to look around for such a place, but the Lord said to me to concentrate with the work; the house would come later. Since then I was "pregnant" with this vision. I learned to prophesy and speak life into it, knowing that at the right time it would come to pass. I knew this would be an "Isaac;" totally from God so that the glory would go to Him! I just kept thanking Him, for this was His idea. Finally, on the day my mom died, Sept. 4, 2002, this "baby" was born. On the way to make the funeral arrangements, I suggested that instead of flowers, it would be a good idea for people to donate money to a cause dear to mom's heart. I suggested that the money be given to a Cuban American group that works for Cuba's freedom from communism. I called up a friend involved with this group and the Lord spoke through her. She said, "Maria, are you serious? Your mom would want every donation to go to the kind of work you're doing; preaching the Gospel, praying for the sick, ministering to the poor. I believe the money should go for your work." I was speechless! That was the last thing on my mind! I couldn't even answer! My friend called me back at the funeral home and said that she would have her lawyer draw up the papers right away to form a non-profit corporation so that the money received could be used for the Lord's work. When she asked me "What name do you want to give it?" The answer was natural and easy:

"The Glory of God!" For six years I spoke life into this vision, waiting on God for His good will to be accomplished. Finally, it was "born" and now it needs to grow up. I continue to proclaim my thanksgiving, to prophesy life and fruitfulness, and to decree and declare that God's plan will be accomplished in and through "The Glory of God." For a year now the "Glory of God" has been contributing to the work of evangelization through the preaching of the Gospel and by helping poor African Catholics obtain an education. I know that as I remain faithful, at the right time the Lord will place the "glory" house in my hands. Amen!

Parents, I want to encourage you to decree, declare and prophesy over your childrens' lives and destinies. If the Lord has given you a word, dream or vision regarding your children, believe it and speak it out. We walk by faith. It's important that you proclaim it and speak it out, as something in the spiritual realm is established with our words. There is power in your tongue! (Proverbs 18:21) It takes time for that vision, word or dream to be manifested. If what you see with your physical eyes does not align with what the Lord has told you, do not establish the negative by constantly repeating your children's failures. Keep believing and speaking forth the Lord's plan for your child, not the enemy's plan. For example, I know my daughter has a prophet's calling on her life. However, this has not yet been manifested in the natural. In the meantime I keep believing and speaking and declaring God's plan for her life. I must admit that at times, when I have focused at the circumstances, I have wondered if I have heard correctly! Recently someone was praying for me and she said that she saw in a vision "my mantle" fall upon my daughter. She believed that my daughter will one day "walk" in my footsteps. I believe this word came from the throne of God to encourage me to keep believing and speaking out God's plan for my daughter! Amen!

The Lord wants to use us to speak and proclaim life into other people's destinies. The prophetic gifts of the Holy Spirit are meant to be used to encourage and "push" people into their calling and destiny. In a recent trip to Nicaragua I was ministering in a church and the Lord gave me a word of knowledge for someone named "Kevin." Kevin identified himself; he was about 10 or 11 years old! I was expecting to see an adult! I prophesied over Kevin, used my tongue to decree and declare what the Lord was putting in my heart, and he rested in the Spirit. Before the trip was over, Kevin was not only speaking in tongues, but also prophesying! It was touching to see a child prophesying with such boldness to the congregation! I believe the Lord has great plans for Kevin!

In Uganda I preached in a prayer group in Kampala. A lady came for prayer. Money that was owed to her, that belonged to her, was not being released as promised. We prayed in agreement (Matthew 18:19) and took authority over the enemy and commanded him to release the money, in the name of Jesus. I "decreed" and "declared" that this money would be released soon into her hands. We asked God for justice. Ps. 103:6 says that:

" The Lord works vindication and justice for all who are oppressed."

A few days later she approached me with a big smile on her face to tell me that she had received her money. Thank you, Jesus! This should not surprise us, for the Lord says in Isaiah 44:26 that He:

"confirms the word of His servant and performs the counsel of His messengers...." Amen.

In a conference in Masaka, Uganda, the Lord gave me a word for those that were looking for work; that jobs would be available for them. I declared that some would go back home and have a job. The news reached me a few days later that a lady who was at the conference, had a job by the time she returned home. She was in awe because she said she was the least qualified for that job and she was the one that was hired! Thank you, Jesus! But isn't our Heavenly Father the owner of every corporation and every job?

# LAUGH!

"…and she laughs at the time to come." Proverbs 31:25b

As we wait on the Lord and are walking by faith, we can laugh before we see the promise with our eyes. Jesus laughs; Ps2:4 says:

"He who sits in the heavens laughs…."

The Lord is not worried about the outcome of our trials because He already knows the end and He can do all things but fail; even if we make mistakes He certainly works them for good (Romans 8:28). What the enemy means for evil the Lord changes for our good and His glory. There is no power shortage in God.

"His hand is not shortened, that it cannot save, or his ear dull that it cannot hear…" (Isaiah 59: 1).

The righteous woman of Proverbs 31 has no problem with laughter; she is not afraid of what the future holds because she knows God. If you think about it, laughter is in our "spiritual DNA" because the name Isaac means laughter (Genesis 21:6). Abraham, the father of our faith, named his child Isaac. Laughter is even good for our bodies!

"A cheerful heart is a good medicine, but a downcast spirit dries up the bones." (Pro.17:22)

Jesus was anointed with "the oil of gladness" beyond anyone else. (Hebrews 1:9) That means that joy was all over Him! This joy gave Him strength and endurance to go through every trial and obstacle, because the "joy of the Lord is our strength." (Nehemiah 8:10) Hebrews 12:2 says about Jesus:

" for the joy that was set before him endured the cross…."

One of the things that the Lord wants to give us is the oil of gladness; it's part of His ministry to us. Isaiah 61:3 says that He wants to give to those who mourn:

"a garland instead of ashes, the oil of gladness instead of mourning; the mantle of praise instead of a faint spirit; that they may be called oaks of righteousness, the planting of the Lord, that He may be glorified."

To live in the joy of the Lord doesn't mean that there are no troubles or suffering in your life; it just means that God is with you and present. Actually, being in the Lord and committed to Him will bring new troubles in our lives! When we lived in darkness the enemy didn't have to worry about us; but now that we are in the light, he will try to destroy our lives (John 10:10) because we have become a threat to him. The Apostle Paul says in 2 Timothy 3:12:

"Indeed, all who desire to live a godly life in Christ Jesus will be persecuted...."

Peter says in 1Peter 4:12:

"Beloved, do not be surprised at the fiery ordeal which comes upon you to prove you, as though something strange were happening to you...."

The point that I want to make is this: there is a godly way to respond to the persecution, criticism and mockery that will come against us, and it's not by retaliating! God's way is this: when it happens, REJOICE! Peter continues in verses 13-14

"...rejoice in so far as you share Christ's sufferings, that you may also rejoice and be glad when His glory is revealed. If you are reproached for the name of Christ, you are blessed, because the spirit of glory and of God rests upon you."

When you come under attack because of Jesus (not because you're a pain!), realize that the Holy Spirit, the spirit of glory, is resting upon you. Don't miss the opportunity to rejoice in the Lord and have fellowship with His Spirit. Remember the blind man in John 9, whose sight Jesus restored? After the miraculous healing the Pharisees came hard upon the man "and cast him out." (v.34) Verses 35-38 say "Jesus heard that they had cast him out, and having found him he said, 'Do you believe in the Son of Man?' He answered, 'And who is he, sir, that I may believe in him?' Jesus said to him, 'You have seen him, and it is he who speaks to you.' He said, 'Lord, I believe'; and he worshipped Him." This is so powerful, because Jesus searched for the man and found him just after he was cast out. The healed man went from the revelation of just knowing the healing power of Jesus to the revelation of knowing Him personally as the Son of Man, and then he worshipped Him. The Pharisees cast him out of their synagogue, but Jesus took him in into His family! Imagine this man's joy, not only for his healing, but that he had come face to face with the King of Glory! Jesus Himself says in Luke 6:22-23:

> "Blessed are you when men hate you, and when they exclude you and revile you, and cast out your name as evil, on account of the Son of man! REJOICE in that day, and LEAP FOR JOY, for behold, your reward is great in heaven; for so their fathers did to the prophets."

I well remember how some of my friends made fun of me when I came to Jesus; mockingly, they would say things like, "Look at her, she's just like the Virgin Mary." I learned to rejoice when they made fun of me, knowing that the Lord was "extra close" in those moments! I figured, "I must be doing something right and the enemy doesn't like it!" Will you, right now, stop reading and start praising Him?

The joy of the Holy Spirit is not dependent on circumstances or other people. The Holy Spirit Himself, as we yield to Him, releases His joy in our lives regardless of what we are going through, because He is the spirit of joy. Galatians 5:22 names joy as a fruit of the Holy Spirit. If you have the Holy Spirit there is joy inside of you. What does joy sound like? Ha, ha, ha, ha! And the Lord wants our joy to be full! (John 15:11) We need His joy, because it is our strength! (Nehemiah 8:10) Experiencing His joy as we wait for the promise will keep us strong in the delay.

Look at what happened in Pentecost when the Holy Spirit came down on the 120 gathered in the upper room (Acts 2). Apparently, they were so filled with joy and laughter that the people outside thought they were drunk. Peter addressed the crowd and told them "...these men are not drunk, as you suppose, since it is only the third hour of the day...(9:00a.m.). (v.15)   We know what "drunk" people look like; they are loud, they laugh, they walk weird, etc. And this is how God's people looked like when the Holy Spirit came on them! Hardly the behavior of "respectable" and "dignified" citizens! The Church was birthed in an atmosphere of joy! As Christians we should be the most joyful of people because truly our God has displayed His love for us powerfully! He is a faithful God! We are children of the Most High God! We are royalty! Think of the joy present in Mary's visit to Elizabeth as she proclaimed the greatness of Her God:

"My soul magnifies the Lord, and my spirit rejoices in God my Savior... for He who is mighty has done great things for me and holy is His name." (Luke 1:46-49)

This encounter between the cousins was hardly a meeting of "dry bones!" (Ezekiel 37) When the shepherds were told by an angel of the Lord about the birth of Jesus, he said to them (Luke 2:10-11), "Be not afraid; for behold, I bring you good news of a great JOY which will come to all the people; for to you is born this day in the city of David a Savior, who is Christ the Lord." The "Good News" is news of joy in season and out of season! What a witness we give to the world when they see us with joy and laughter even in the midst of a dark world!   When the Lord delivered His people out of bondage in Egypt,

"He led forth His people with joy, his chosen ones with singing." (Ps. 105:43) Amen!

The first time I went to a charismatic prayer group one of the things that really touched me was to see the joy of the people. These people were actually rejoicing! I was "lost" and could not understand why they were so happy; but I wanted what I saw in them. I was miserable even though I had everything the world had to offer. I was joyless. Today I've had people walk up to me and tell me that they want "what I have." If you watch people's faces most are depressed, anxious and upset. As God's people, spending time in His presence will transform us into the image of Jesus (2 Cor. 3:18) and the joy and laughter will flow through us because "there is fullness of joy" in the presence of the Lord (Ps. 16:II). I believe this is one of the reasons why Pope John Paul II is exhorting us to contemplate the face of Christ. Ultimately, we become what we look at. The Apostle Paul says in 2 Cor. 317-18:

"Now the Lord is the Spirit, where the Spirit of the Lord is, there is freedom. And we all, with unveiled face, beholding the glory of the Lord, are being changed into His likeness from one degree of glory to another; for this comes from the Lord who is the Spirit."

Will you quit looking at your problems and start looking at the Lord? You will be changed! The prophet Isaiah says in chapter 60:1-2:

"Arise, shine; for your light has come, and the glory of the Lord has risen upon you. For behold, darkness shall cover the earth, and thick darkness the peoples; but the Lord will arise upon you and His glory will be seen upon you."

In the midst of a dark and lost world, we are different because His light and His glory shine upon us. We are joyful and not depressed, walking in His strength, wisdom and power! This will attract the lost to us so that we can lead them to Jesus Christ. Amen!

# III. GOD'S FAITHFULNESS

"Therefore know that the Lord your God,
He is God, the faithful God who keeps
Covenant and mercy for a thousand
Generations with those who love Him
And keep His commandments...." (Deuteronomy 7:9)

## HE REMEMBERS!

"For He remembered his holy promise...." (Ps. 105:42)

We have such a faithful God! All throughout Scripture we see Him remembering and being faithful to His people.

"The steadfast love of the Lord never ceases, His mercies never come to an end; they are new every morning; great is thy faithfulness." (Lamentations 3:22-23)

With God every day is a new beginning. He never runs out of mercy! There's a fresh supply every morning! If you have been serving the Lord and discouragement has set in, listen to what He says in Hebrews 6:10:

"For God is not so unjust as to overlook your work and the love which you showed for His sake in serving the saints, as you still do."

He keeps account of even the smallest demonstrations of love and concern for His people:

"And whoever gives to one of these little ones even a cup of cold water because he is a disciple, truly, I say to you, he shall not lose his reward." (Matthew 10:42)

*109*

"God remembered Noah" (Genesis 8:1) and through him the human race was able to continue. Imagine Noah locked up in the ark with all those smelly animals, wondering when the time would come for him to step on solid ground once again. But God had established a covenant with Noah (Genesis 6:18), and He is a covenant-keeping God! It was God himself who shut Noah in the ark (Genesis7:16). Sometimes we are also shut in a situation with no way out, but the Lord will remember, and at the right time He will lead us out.

God also remembered Abraham, His friend, when he was about to destroy Sodom (Genesis 19:29). Abraham's nephew, Lot, and his two daughters were saved from destruction thanks to Abraham's intercession (Genesis 18:17-33). God had established a covenant with Abraham also (Genesis 17:4); not only with him but with his descendants:

> "And I will establish my covenant between me and you and your descendants after you throughout their generations for an everlasting covenant, to be God to you and to your descendants after you." (v.7)

When we pray and stand in intercession for others, God will also remember us, and at the right time He will intervene! For years in our prayer group we had been interceding for the salvation of a dear sister's husband. He didn't want anything to do with Jesus; we shared the Gospel with him and he said that he just couldn't "believe." He had never allowed his wife to send the children to Catholic schools nor receive any religious education. She was able to baptize her children and that was about it. The daughter made her first Holy Communion when she got married! He was "anti-Church." His health started to deteriorate, and still no sign of repentance. However, we have a faithful God! Recently he told his wife that he wanted to turn to Jesus and they prayed together proclaiming Jesus as Lord and Savior. We called a Charismatic priest from my parish who ministered to him. Suddenly, all those prayers on his behalf were answered! God "remembered!" What joy we have in our hearts to see our friend's husband turn to the

Lord! We rejoice in His faithfulness!

When the Jews were in bondage in Egypt for hundreds of years,

"God heard their groaning, and God remembered his covenant with Abraham, with Isaac, and with Jacob. And God saw the people of Israel, and God knew their condition." (Exodus 2:24-25)

God was faithful to his promise and sent Moses to deliver them. Ps. 136: 23-24 says:

"It is He who remembered us in our low estate, for his steadfast love endures for ever; and rescued us from our foes, for his steadfast love endures for ever."

Rachel, Jacob's favorite wife, was not able to have children and she was desperate; but:

"God remembered Rachel, and God hearkened to her and opened her womb." (Genesis 30:22)

In 1 Samuel 1, we see Hannah miserable because she too is unable to conceive and have a child. She poured her heart to the Lord and made a vow to Him "O Lord of hosts, if thou wilt indeed look on the affliction of thy maidservant, and remember me, and not forget they maidservant, but wilt give to thy maidservant a son, then I will give him to the Lord all the days of his life...." (v.11) In verses 19 –20 we read that her husband:

"...knew Hannah his wife, and the Lord remembered her;
and in due time Hannah conceived and bore a son, and she called his name Samuel, for she said "I have asked him of the Lord."

Sometimes people say that "the Lord has forgotten me." Nothing could be further from the truth. This is God's answer to that comment:

> "Can a woman forget her suckling child, that she should have no compassion on the son of her womb? Even these may forget, yet I will not forget you. Behold, I have graven you on the palms of my hands; your walls are continually before me." (Isaiah 49: 15-16)

Ps. 103:13-14 says:

> "As a father pities his children, so that Lord pities those who fear Him. For He knows our frame; He remembers we are dust."

Of all the things that God remembers, there is nothing more precious than the Blood of the Covenant of the Lord Jesus Christ. This is the covenant of our salvation. Jesus paid the price for us with His blood. It's His blood that caused the curtain in the Temple to be torn; the curtain that kept humanity from the presence of God. (Matthew 27:51) Now it's through His blood that we have access into God's presence. His blood shed for our redemption is the only acceptable sacrifice that satisfies the Father for our sins. Ephesians 1:7 says:

> "In Him we have redemption through His blood, the forgiveness of our trespasses...."

Hebrews 9:22 says:

> "...without the shedding of blood there is no forgiveness of sins."

Hebrews 7:25 says:

> "Consequently He is able for all time to save those who

draw near to God through Him since He always lives to make intercession for them."

The Apostle Paul says in Romans 10:9-11:

"....if you confess with your lips that Jesus is Lord and believe in your heart that God raised Him from the dead, you will be saved. For man believes with his heart and so is justified, and he confesses with his lips and so is saved. The Scripture says, 'No one who believes in Him will be put to shame'."

If you have never trusted Jesus for your salvation and eternal life, and you have a desire to do so, please say this prayer out loud:

"Father God, I come before you now as a repentant sinner. I realize that I'm guilty and that I need your forgiveness and salvation. Lord Jesus, I believe You are the Son of God. I believe you died for me on the Cross of Calvary and paid the penalty for all my sins. I ask You now to forgive me all my sins; wash me, cleanse me, with your precious Blood and make me white as snow. I confess with my mouth that Jesus is Lord and I transfer my trust for my salvation upon His finished work at the Cross. I believe that He rose from the dead and is now seated at the right hand of the Father, interceding for me. Thank you Lord, for the gift of salvation and eternal life. Fill me with your Holy Spirit to live out the new life in victory! Thank you, Jesus. Amen!"

# GOD WORKS "SUDDENLY"

"Admire not how sinners live, but trust in the Lord and wait for His light; For it is easy with the Lord suddenly, in an instant, to make a poor man rich." (Sirach 11:21-22) (NAB)

As God's people we don't have to despair or become hopeless or think that He has forgotten us, for He works "suddenly." Our God is never late, although He rarely shows up when we want Him to! On Pentecost Day, Acts 2:2:

"suddenly"

the Holy Spirit came and all were filled with the Holy Spirit and spoke in other tongues. Aren't you glad that the 120 followers of Jesus "waited" for the promise of the Father to be "clothed with power from on high?" (Luke 24:49) As Saul of Tarsus, the great persecutor of the church, approached Damascus to apprehend more Christians,

"suddenly"

a light from the sky blinded him. He fell and heard the voice of Jesus. Forever he was changed (Acts 9:3-4). When Paul and Silas were imprisoned in Philippi (Acts 16:25-26), they were praising the Lord at the midnight hour when

"suddenly"

a severe earthquake shook the place. The prison doors were opened and "everyone's chains were pulled loose." In Luke 2:13, as the shepherds were having another boring night with the sheep,

"suddenly"

a multitude of the heavenly host appeared praising God. As Jesus was being baptized in the Jordan,

"suddenly"

the heavens opened and the Holy Spirit descended and hovered over Him (Matt. 3:16). (NAB) In John 6:21, after the multiplication of bread, the disciples found themselves trying to cross by boat to Capernaum. They rowed and rowed getting nowhere because the wind was strong and the sea was rough. After Jesus came to them walking on the sea,

"suddenly"

they reached shore. (NAB) On the Mount of Transfiguration

"suddenly"

Moses and Elijah appeared conversing with Jesus. (Matthew 17:3- NAB)

After I got the revelation of God's sudden moves, I started to pray for "suddenlies." In the year of the Jubilee, my son Victor "suddenly" said yes to my invitation for a retreat. So many times he had told me that he couldn't make it. My friend's lump on her hand "suddenly" disappeared as the power of the Holy Spirit was released on her. Recently in Nicaragua, we prayed with a family for the Lord to "suddenly" move and have their relative released from prison. A week and half later I received an e-mail that this man had been "suddenly" released from prison. The Lord put a desire in my heart to preach in Africa; a month after this I "suddenly" received an invitation to proclaim the good news on this continent. I remember waiting for two months for the judge's decision in my court case, when "suddenly" the phone rang and the news of victory resounded in my ears! On the day my mother passed away, "suddenly," the "Glory of God" was born.

If you're waiting on God, and you're in the midst of a "delay," He will move suddenly! Just at the right time!

Dear reader, I pray that this book has been an instrument in the hands of the Holy Spirit to encourage you as you press into your "destiny." It's the purpose of this book to strengthen your faith and adjust your vision so that you DO NOT GIVE UP! The Lord is raising an army of believers to carry out His purposes. You are one of them! Every tear, trial and testing that you have gone through is worth it! There is a "crown of life" that awaits you. James says

> "Blessed is the man who endures trial, for when he has stood the test he will receive the crown of life which God has promised to those who love Him." (James 1:12)

What a privilege to be a child of God and to serve Him! I believe we have "chosen the good portion" and it shall not be taken away from us (Luke 10:42)!

> "But, as it is written, "What no eye has seen, nor ear heard,
> nor the heart of man conceived, what God has prepared for those who love Him..." (1 Corinthians 2:9).

Remember, we are "more than conquerors through Him who loved us!"(Romans 8:37) Let's declare, like Job, that

> "...when He has tried me, I shall come forth as gold." (Job 23:10) Amen!